Antiracism and Universal Design for Learning

Building Expressways to Success

BY ANDRATESHA FRITZGERALD

FOREWORD BY SAMARIA RICE,
MOTHER OF TAMIR RICE

CAST | Until learning has no limits·

For Tamir Rice.
You will never be forgotten.
We will fight for your light to shine, always.

Table of Contents

Foreword by Samaria Rice

As the founder and CEO of the Tamir Rice Foundation, Samaria Rice advocates for juvenile rights to honor her 12-year-old son, who was fatally shot by Cleveland police in 2014.

I've learned to question just about everything when it comes to society's view of our Black babies. The tragic murder of my son Tamir Rice sent shockwaves throughout the United States and beyond. Tamir Rice is now a global public figure. Why? Because communities all over the world could see the tragedy of what happens when white supremacy is enacted in law enforcement. Our community mourned with me as power and privilege reared their ugly heads and devastated my family.

This type of violence birthed in racism—in a country that has a bitter history of slavery, lynchings, and stealing black souls from Africa—takes place not only in the corrupt system of policing in a white privileged society. Sadly, this scenario plays out too many times to count in classrooms in America. For this reason, the fight for justice and equality must extend beyond police and criminal justice reform. It must include how people are treated in stores and restaurants, in public spaces, in government offices, and in houses of worship. And it must extend to schools and other places of learning, such as preschools and colleges, where our young people spend huge parts of their day.

Oppressive systems built on white supremacy put obstacles in the road for our Black children. These obstacles shut down the way that Black children learn and express themselves to their full potential. My son Tamir was an all-American Black child who loved many things. He loved basketball, soccer, riding his bike, helping younger and older people, and drawing. These were some positive ways he expressed himself. Physical activity was a beautiful part of the way that he was wired to shine. How many hours did he spend in school being told to sit down, sit still, be quiet?

To achieve success in a traditional school setting, Black children are disrespected by authority and asked to conform, comply, and compartmentalize their identities, their uniqueness, and their beauty. Our children have been slammed by security guards and led out in handcuffs by police officers. I cringe when I read stories of students being brutalized with ultimatums to either cut their dreadlocks or be excluded from activities. I shake my head in disbelief that laws have to be passed to protect Black people from being discriminated against due to their hairstyles. Schools have to become safe relationally and emotionally for Black children before they can be safe academically.

In 2020, when I now write, protesters have taken to the streets across the United States—and in many countries throughout the world—to condemn police brutality and the unjust use of deadly force. They have declared, resoundingly, that until Black Lives Matter everywhere, justice is not possible anywhere.

The racism and outrageous abuse of power that resulted in the deaths of Ahmaud Arbery, Breonna Taylor, George Floyd, that of my son Tamir Rice, and of countless other African American victims in just the past decade at the hands of this oppressive system—these travesties don't just spring out of the nowhere. They are the most visible examples of the deadly, dehumanizing effects of racism that Black and Brown people experience every day in countless ways, big and small. If we looked at educational assaults due to racism and inequity, how many names would we have to add to the ledger of tragedy?

I want to take a moment to speak directly to the educators who care enough to change the trajectory of success of Black children in America. Here is a pop quiz for you. What is your motive for teaching, especially in urban communities? Do you expect to transmit content without actively seeking a personal relationship with students and families? You have to have a relationship so that parents know what to expect and teachers know the expectations of parents. This is what partnership looks like. I wish these things were included in preservice teaching programs. Will you commit to connecting with the community, addressing the social needs, and deconstructing racist structures to lift up Black students?

Please understand that I have a responsibility to demand these answers for different and better results. Our babies have to succeed! Honest conversations need to happen.

I had the intellectual and emotional savvy to survive in the streets on my own from the age of 12. I knew a whole lot about life, even as a child. We cannot miss these opportunities for children to bring all of themselves and their whole story into the classroom. They bring their full story every time they step foot in the school building. Is your classroom set up to acknowledge their story or ignore it?

So as you prepare to read this book, remember my questions. Remember my story. Remember my son Tamir and his siblings, Tasheona, Tavon, Tajai, and all the children who look like them. The issues we are facing in this world demand that educators drop their defenses and deliver a high-quality education in the way that every child needs and deserves.

Are you ready to recognize these areas of challenge and pick up the mantle of opportunity?

Are you ready to admit that Black and Brown children have been geniuses sitting in broken systems that are not built to see the brilliance they bring?

Are you ready to fight against mindsets that prioritize policing over educational practices that lead to a life of freedom?

Are you ready to partner with parents and families in a meaningful way by valuing our hopes and dreams for our own babies?

Are you ready to admit that teaching practices are broken and that many Black babies have been labeled and overidentified because educational systems haven't wanted to face this truth?

I've earned the right to question just about everything when it comes to society's view of our Black babies. Just as I fought for my children to receive the best education and for every teacher assigned to my children to work with me for my children—my fight continues.

Racism has no place in this world. It surely has no place in schools.

That's why this book from Andratesha Fritzgerald is so important. From her lifetime of experience as a student of color in our schools and universities and now as a teacher and administrator, she knows firsthand the ways in which systemic racism communicates to Black and Brown students every day that they are participating in a system built for others, one that values white experiences, cultures, history, language, families, communities, work schedules, and achievements above all else. But unlike a lot of books which simply document these injustices, Andratesha Fritzgerald recommends a positive and proactive approach that educators can take to undo the everyday racism of schools.

She begins with the essential idea of Honor. Every Black and Brown student should know that their experiences are a valuable basis for further learning. They should know that they are people who deserve the very best education we can offer, one that respects their cultures and communities and prepares them for the life they are destined to live.

Fritzgerald offers very practical suggestions for making inclusion, antiracism, and the acceptance of differences the first step and most important step in lesson planning. Even though the focus in her book is antiracism, I love that Universal Design for Learning (UDL) began as a way to include students with disabilities and other learning differences in the general education curriculum. So many Black and Brown students are labeled and segregated in special education tracks not because they are disabled but because they are different. UDL, the way Andratesha Fritzgerald practices it, is a way to remedy that.

This book gives me hope that in education we can begin to eliminate the violence of academic and social prejudice that kills the spirit of our babies and belittles the needs and experiences of people of color. Because we cannot forget the days of slavery when Black people were not allowed to read and write—we have to take the chains off of education in every way today.

In the movie *The Great Debaters*, the character Samantha ends her emotional speech about race relations with these words: "The time for justice, the time for freedom, and the time for equality is always right now!" I could not agree more!

Teachers, read this book. Answer the questions. Create the partnerships. I'm counting on you to do the work and make change for the better. Are you willing and ready to stand with me for Black students? Until Black Students Matter, no students truly do.

Now is the time. Now is *your* time. Right now.

Prologue: Invitation to "Good Trouble"

The word antiracist carries with it a punch that demands attention. It is easy to see the need for antiracism when we look at the horrors of slavery or look back at the Civil Rights movement of the Sixties. It is more difficult to see the strongholds of racism that are embedded as tradition or practices that have been the bedrock of schooling for as long as any of us can remember. Because these systems are so strongly pinned to our experiences and many people's definition of what's "right," there is much antiracism work needed.

When we look at data that tells us that Black students are suspended at a rate that is three times higher than their white counterparts—we know that antiracism work is needed.

When we see that there is evidence that shows Black students are either overidentified for special education or underserved because of the color of their skin—we know that antiracism work is needed.

When Black and Brown students are systematically denied access to gifted and advanced placement courses—we have all the evidence we need that antiracism work is needed.

Racist systems still exist and need to be acknowledged and dismantled so that all learners will experience the freedom of learning without barriers. It's time for a revival in our schools. It's time for a celebration at the place where effort meets innovation. It's time to make some of that "good trouble" that the late Civil Rights hero, John Lewis, talked about. We need a revival that makes sense for our schools, our families, and our Black and Brown children. This book will help teachers and leaders proactively name and eliminate barriers—academic, behavioral, social, and emotional barriers—and to also address and eliminate institutional racism in our systems and schools.

Thank you for being willing to set out on this journey.

Antiracism and UDL Begin with Honor

Thirty students in a classroom. Eight could breeze through the content with or without the instructor. Another four need a bit of a push but eventually grasp the content. A few succeed with the help of special education supports. The remaining learners "just don't get it," according to the teacher.

Cherish—female, thriving—is part of the first group. She loves school. She comes into class daily ready to learn, eager to read, raising her hand, sharing her thoughts. She feels like a winner. Her grades reflect that message back to her. But she is pregnant and afraid that she soon won't be able to keep the secret she has hidden for five whole months.

Across the room sits Deacon—male, surviving but barely. He's part of the group that supposedly doesn't get it. He tries to hide. His goal is to disappear by pretending to complete an assignment he can't read. He avoids contact with the other students unless, for some reason, he has to deflect, defend, distract. He feels like a failure. His grades reflect that message in that class. The teacher has no clue that Deacon leaves school and works until midnight since his father has become disabled.

Every week, the same students are fabulous, the same students fail, the same students are lost, the same students get labeled. The teacher, with best intentions, makes a general announcement. "Hey, if you aren't happy with your grade I will be here after school. Some of you are failing, and I haven't seen you show up after school yet. I'm here if you need me."

Yet he has no idea of the struggles his students face every day and how heavily the system is stacked against these brilliant minds. He does not know for sure who is homeless, who is hungry, who is afraid of being jumped, who has moved 17 times in two years, who is being molested, who is addicted, who is being prostituted, who is listening, or who needs someone to listen. The teacher is satisfied with business as usual because he offered "help." He has no idea that staying after-school might interfere with caring for a sibling or working to pay bills. He doesn't realize that walking home alone after dark is a life or death dilemma. With no transportation options, few support networks, and real-life challenges, the students who need his help must refuse it to truly help and protect themselves.

They prioritize and so does the teacher. What is most important? Who is most important? Sometimes we tout mission statements, vision statements, and goals that include buzzwords that everyone says and everyone can recite but only a few actually live the words out. You can tell what is most important by the student achievement. You can tell who is most important by who is achieving the most. And what about the ones who are not achieving? Both students get up when the bell rings and race to Mrs. Jackson's class on the other side of the building.

In 2015, the US Department of Education's Civil Rights Data reported that 12 percent of Black students were held back in ninth grade, while just 4 percent of white students were, according to US News & World Report (Cook, 2015). Across all grades, Black students were nearly three times more likely to be held back as their white peers. Small wonder, then, that Black students were also more likely to drop out of high school before getting a diploma.

I can't help but think of seven-year-old Linda Carol Brown walking block after block to the bus stop to ride to her all-Black school two miles from home because she was not allowed to attend a white school just four blocks away. We are sure there was someone who stood and proclaimed, in the tone of *Plessy v. Ferguson*, that separate schools were "pretty good considering"—or at least good enough for "those kids." Just good enough is not good enough until it is good for all students, including our brilliant Black and Brown students.

Now let's envision Cherish and Deacon in another class—one that is both universally designed and antiracist.

Deacon loves the music-video parody the teacher debuts to her class before posting to her YouTube channel. He sits at the architectural drawing table and pulls out his materials. Mrs. Jackson asks him when their next check-in is scheduled. "Next Tuesday," he says with a laugh. "But I might need more time because I saw some stuff I want to add to my crib."

Mrs. Jackson is aware of Deacon's situation so she encouraged him to attend the class, but he has an alternative course of study through a credit flexibility syllabus they created together. She knows that he uses geometry every day because he learned how to rehab homes from his Dad before the illness. Even though he can eyeball an angle and cut a corresponding one freehand, he has been having a hard time keeping pace with content that is far beneath his ability.

"This gonna be nice," he brags a bit.

"Well, nice," says Mrs. Jackson. "Better consult those guidelines for the final project. Make sure each milestone is reached. At the check-in come prepared with questions and samples. We might have to see about building this house for me." They laugh.

Each student is using this structured study day to either cultivate curiosity, build on questions, inquire about concepts they are unsure of, or review their peers, projects in progress.

Cherish is on the computer with her headphones and smacks her lips in annoyance at the laughter between Mrs. Jackson and Deacon. She is watching the prerecorded tutorial and preparing to tackle a problem before creating one for a friend she is swapping with.

"I need to make sure I get this before . . . you know," she says as she points to the computer screen.

Mrs. Jackson says, "Cherish, turn the volume up on those headphones and get down to business." They share a secret knowing smile, and Mrs. Jackson places a note in her hand that she was writing while they were speaking to one another. The note simply says, "There is someone who will be looking up to you. Don't let her down (or him if the baby is a boy.)" Cherish folds up the note, smiles, and adjusts the volume.

She exchanges three problems with her classmate instead of one because they want to make sure they understand the concept well enough to teach it. The standard does not change because of situations or hardships. The standard is communicated, and the road to reach the standard is paved with flexibility.

Regardless of the color of skin, disability, socioeconomic status, or home situation, antiracist teaching demands excellence in a way that communicates honor to the learner. What is the difference between offering help and designing a course that is helpful to every student? What makes the difference is *honor*. The notion of honor is important to the successful implementation of UDL. Honor is most often communicated in the actions that answer the question, "Who is most important?"

Lisa Delpit (1988), a pioneering writer in the field of education and antiracism, writes that an important first step toward antiracist teaching is recognizing the codes of power that operate in the classroom. She proposes five aspects of power that both teachers and students should be aware of:

1. Issues of power are enacted in the classroom.

2. There are codes or rules for participating in power; that is, there is a "culture of power."

3. The rules of the culture of power are a reflection of the rules of the culture of those who have power.

4. If you are not already a participant in the culture of power, being told explicitly the rules of that culture makes acquiring power easier.

5. Those with power are frequently least aware of—or least willing to acknowledge—its existence. Those with less power are often most aware of its existence.

On the last point, Delpit says: "Acknowledging personal power and admitting participation in a culture of power is distinctly uncomfortable" (p. 26). This culture of power aims to protect the status quo. The culture of power is assimilationist—not antiracist. For that reason, Delpit encourages teachers and students to openly discuss these codes of power and how they operate: "The teacher cannot be the only expert in the classroom. To deny students their own expert knowledge is to disempower them" (p. 32).

Antiracist learning environments are not built around a "savior complex" of rescuing Black and Brown children from the ills of the world. When a learning environment is truly antiracist then all learners will be empowered beyond bias to make decisions about their learning and leading because the environment is welcoming and safe. Creating culturally responsive, culturally sustaining, flexible and empowering classrooms distributes the power that is traditionally held by the teacher and releases those who have had power in them all along to shine. Tradition has upheld racist values that hold the genius of Black and Brown children hostage to white rhetoric. Honor places learners in the driver's seat.

Honor says, "I see you. I am learning from you. I acknowledge you. You are welcome here. You belong. Your success is my mission." The codes of power that dishonor students speak to the need to create a new code—a more inclusive and empowering code. Where power was once the stronghold controlled solely by the teachers, I am proposing a new code. A code of honor. There are five elements to establishing and acting upon the code of honor that are juxtaposed to Delpit's assertions:

1. Recognize the power structure that exists—both past and present.

2. Acknowledge the purposeful intent and actions of abolishing the limitations of the power structure at hand.

3. Reflect the code of honor by empowering each member of the learning community daily in the structures, supports and choices available.

4. Make an effort to invite members of the learning community into positions of authority, power, and decision making—even if that means taking yourself out of power to do so.

5. Create opportunities for members of the learning community to make powerful decisions that govern their best possible outcomes.

When these five elements of honor are enacted in our learning environments, we will see a shift in the status quo. When schools and learning communities become places where all students can exercise their power and eliminate the learned powerlessness, the code of honor will take over the code of power. When success is not just a gatekeeper's exam but rather a personalized road to the path that is chosen by the student—this is honor. When school success is demystified for all students of all races and all abilities and all backgrounds—especially for our Black and Brown students who are the furthest from educational justice—then the codes of power will be broken and the code of honor will elevate each student to the status of learner and leader.

Table 1.1: A Crosswalk of Delpit's Codes of Power and Fritzgerald's Codes of Honor

Codes of Power (Delpit, 1988)	Codes of Honor (Fritzgerald, 2020)
Issues of power are enacted in the classroom.	Recognize the power structure that exists—both past and present.
There are codes or rules for participating in power; that is, there is a "culture of power."	Acknowledge the purposeful intent and actions of abolishing the limitations of the power structure at hand.
The rules of the culture of power are a reflection of the rules of the culture of those who have power.	Reflect the code of honor by empowering each member of the learning community daily in the structures, supports and choices available.
If you are not already a participant in the culture of power, being told explicitly the rules of that culture makes acquiring power easier.	Make an effort to invite members of the learning community into positions of authority, power, and decision making—even if that means taking yourself out of power to do so.
Those with power are frequently least aware of—or least willing to acknowledge—its existence. Those with less power are often most aware of its existence.	Create opportunities for members of the learning community to make powerful decisions that govern their best possible outcomes.

Ahram et al. (2011) put it this way: "The capacity for developing students' familiarity with the codes of power has to be taught explicitly and thoughtfully incorporated into the fabric of all core instructional offerings so that it will create an internal value to school success for students that does not contradict other critical dimensions of themselves."

Think back to the classroom scenarios at the beginning of the chapter and reflect on the following questions.

- Can you point out the power?

- Can you point out the honor?

- Who is most important?

- Is it the teacher, who services the students to the level that he is satisfied or the one who is not satisfied until all students learn?

- Is it the students who are passing the course with flying colors because all of the conditions meet their individual needs without intervention?

- Is it the students who are maintaining a passing grade because the help they are receiving meets their needs?

- Is it the students who are often off task? Is it the special education students who are treated as one group regardless of their disability?

- Is it the students who "don't get it?"

- Who is the *most* important?

From the outside looking in it is comfortable to address issues of power and honor, but the uncomfortable stance is the one that changes the view. Are you willing to reconsider your own power, privilege, and practice to truly honor the students you serve? Are you willing to look at the consequences of staying the same? If we do nothing to change, then we are practicing dishonor of Black and Brown children. If we do nothing, we are encouraging their failure and embracing a system that has proven to be racist for as long as schooling has been in existence. Antiracism must be active, not passive. Universal Design for Learning has to be intentionally implemented—not just intended. Success for all must be more than passion. Power by empowerment! This work does not just depend on what we know in terms of content or statistics, it depends on what we do. What actions beyond self-examination are you willing to take?

You are reading this book because you are committed to lifting up your Black and Brown students. You are a part of the renewal movement, searching for solutions instead of admiring the problem. You are a member of the "whatever it takes" tribe to see students thrive regardless of academic and non-academic barriers. You are the ones that will point out the power, snatch it, lay it down to elevate those who have been disenfranchised and made to believe they are voiceless and choiceless. You are not content with saying, "I'm not racist." You are ready to work against systems of racist rhetoric and build universally designed learning environments that demand excellence by honoring all!

Many schools have classrooms in which both scenarios exist for different students. Many students walk into learning environments where they are counted out when the teacher has sorted them out into groups of presumed ability. John Hattie, an educational researcher known for his meta-analysis *Visible Learning* (2008), determined that one of the indicators with the highest effect size on the academic achievement of students is their teachers' estimates of achievement. As Killian (2017), points out, "This reflects the accuracy of teachers' knowledge of students in their classes, not 'teacher expectation'." The truth about every student mentioned above is that every single one of them is important but not all of them are being honored.

Honor is the underlying thread that weaves together the pedagogical decision making that leads all students to the education they deserve. If one of the leading factors for student achievement is predicated on teachers' accuracy of knowledge of students in their classes, then as educators we have to be painstakingly sure that the knowledge we are using to make educational decisions is not colored through the lens of bias, racism, or limiting perceptions. Nor should our students' ability or lack of ability be solely determined by one snapshot assessment on one day of one year.

Honor in action begins with a determination to truly help the student become aware of strengths and areas of growth. As educators who honor them, we learn alongside them about their strengths, their areas of giftedness, their goals, their destination, and their definition of success. Without it, we disrespect their path to success based on what we think about them without the honor of knowing for sure that we are preparing them by equipping them to learn beyond barriers.

In *Universal Design for Learning: Theory and Practice*, Meyer, Rose, and Gordon (2014) share an analogy that shows how context can honor or dishonor the learning potential in any student: "Consider any seed as having a fixed or standard potential to grow. However, if you move that seed to Antarctica, does it still retain the same potential to grow? This is an example of the impact of context on growth in learning" (p. 11).

These powerful words lead us to consider the educability of all students. Each student, as a seed, has a right to grow. We honor this right by making our classrooms lush rain forests of opportunities for growth, not vast deserts where growth only a few cacti bloom and all other growth is virtually non-existent. As Sonia Nieto (2004), a distinguished scholar of multiculturalism, writes:

> Our schools reflect the sociocultural and sociopolitical context in which we live. This context is unfair to many young people and their families and the situations in which they live and go to school, but teachers and other educators do not simply have to go along with this reality. I believe one of our primary rules as educators is to interrupt the cycle of inequality and oppression. We can do this best by teaching well and with heart and soul (p. 496).

Embracing the notion of teaching with heart and soul informs the work of the educator. Teaching well with heart and soul honors the student and invigorates the educator by partnering for honor without revoking power from the student.

UDL honors the growth potential by thinking ahead of the learners that educators serve. Again, Meyer, Rose, and Gordon (2014) write:

> From a practical viewpoint, it means that a UDL curriculum designer or teacher can plan for expected variability across learners and provide a curriculum that has corresponding flexibility. The lesson or curriculum should then have the flexibility and affordances to amplify natural abilities and reduce unnecessary barriers for most students and enable teachers to customize easily for each learner (p. 10).

UDL helps us create learning environments that not only prepare us for students' differences but welcome them. It helps us personalize pathways to success for Cherish, Deacon, and all students. We invite more geniuses to the conversation when we allow them to express their brilliance in their natural way of giftedness. The brilliant reader is sitting next to the brilliant rapper who is across from a budding "Gordon Parks" who is right next to the next poet laureate of the United States. UDL honors individual student strengths and lets children communicate their learning through the avenue that best showcases their brilliance!

What about racism? While the UDL Guidelines do not explicitly name racism and other social pathologies as a barrier to learning, they do give educators numerous ways to explicitly address racism and other barriers that Black and Brown children experience. For example, the Guidelines (2018) urge us to "activate or supply background knowledge," "highlight patterns, critical features, big ideas, and relationships," "foster collaboration and community," "vary the methods for response and navigation," "promote expectations and beliefs that optimize motivation," "facilitate personal coping skills and strategies," "heighten salience of goals and objectives," "promote understanding across languages," "optimize relevance, value, and authenticity," and perhaps most important of all: "minimize threats and distractions."

Racism is clearly a threat and distraction to the Black and Brown children who experience it before they have language or knowledge to articulate what they are experiencing. As UDL practitioners, we must have the courage and wisdom to clearly name race as a barrier in our lesson planning. And we must work to create systems that honor our Black and Brown students while providing flexible pathways that are culturally sustaining. Seen through the lens of antiracism, what does it mean to "heighten [the] salience of goals and objectives" or to "optimize relevance, value, and authenticity?" What does it mean for a Black or Brown child to "activate or supply background knowledge," or to "highlight patterns, critical features, big ideas, and relationships?" Are these considerations showing up in your designing? These are essential questions that we need to address when we address the role of racism as a learning barrier.

At this writing the uprisings and unrest in the United States and throughout the world following George Floyd's murder are moving the pendulum toward the truth that Black lives *do* matter. They always have. We must now acknowledge the barriers that have caused children to feel like they can't breathe. Instructional practices that suffocate Black and Brown children with low expectations, or criminalize them, or deny them access to educational opportunities are placing a knee on their neck daily.

We cannot, in good conscience or in good teaching, stand by and watch another generation be marginalized because we don't take action. Inaction is agreement. Inaction is racism. Inaction is injustice. Inaction is inhumane. Inaction is not an option.

Because students are given choices to express themselves, they are constantly reminded that their needs are important to the learning community and to the community at large. Every student is honored by learning opportunities that challenge and support them. In communities where students are honored, we communicate:

- You are more important than the systems we serve.

- You are more important than *my* personal preferences.

- You are more important than the way the content is packaged.

- I am willing to learn about you to help you reach your life goals.

- You are important and I will honor you with instruction that holds you accountable and empowers you to take ownership of your own learning.

There are so many ways to honor our students and our learning community with the work that we do. We can lift our students with the honor that is embedded in the UDL framework, which recognizes and celebrates our differences and the need for flexible learning environments. If we are brave enough to call out the barriers in our system, fight actively to dismantle our system, and commit to being antiracist, we have the power to take action to design something better, something just, something that honors every child as the brilliant scholar they are.

The Urban Teacher's Reality

"Please, Just Keep Teaching"

During my first year of teaching, I was a part of a mentoring program that brought together a small number of teachers from five urban districts in the Cleveland area. The professor who pulled us together shared the sobering statistic that over half of all new teachers leave the profession in just five years. The rates were even higher in urban education. Though the odds seemed to be stacked against young optimistic teachers like us, we gathered every other week to learn new strategies, share dilemmas, vent, and sometimes just cry.

I remember one intern, Matt, sharing a story that reminded me of how different urban education is. Matt's dark eyes seemed eager to share what he must have been carrying with him the entire day. He told us about teaching a science lesson about the DNA "double helix." Matt had a gift for creating highly engaging experiences that gave biology a personality. It was more than a teaching gig for him, it was a chance for him to introduce students to his two loves: acting and science. He had a knack for using literature and experiments to communicate big scientific ideas. He loved questions and reflecting and creating crazy videos. But this day he was serious and concerned. His students were in investigative centers when sirens started blaring close to his classroom window. Shouts and a ruckus followed, meaning that something was happening, and it wasn't good.

While some students situated themselves away from the window and still others dropped to their knees on the floor, one caught Matt's attention. "Teach, Mr. Z. Just keep teaching. I'm sick of stopping every time something is going on. It's the hood! There is always something going on. Just please keep teaching." His voice quieted from a shout to just above a whisper.

The activity outside was still happening, and one of the girls proclaimed "I want to know what's going on" as she made her way to twist the blinds open.

"Hey!" Mr. Z yelled. "Get away from the window and get back to your groups." He said it was a sobering moment for him. "Just keep teaching."

That story has stayed with me for many years. I wrestled with that notion of pausing instruction because of the streets—or the grief or the beef. This is urban education. Content would always take a back seat if circumstances are considered. The sirens are a normal part of our lives. Teachers, leaders, and students alike experience the drama and the trauma of urban education. We know the dangers and the downfalls. We know the success and the strategies. We know the devastation and the celebration. And we know the role of education in the places deemed the darkest and most dangerous in major metropolitan cities.

I remembered thinking, "What would I have done in that situation?" All hell is breaking loose right outside your door and you have one student begging you to keep teaching. The story of that student's voice came to mind each time one of our babies was shot and killed, or when one was arrested for murdering or robbing or stealing. That student's voice came to mind when someone told me they were pregnant, or when deciding to place the call to Children and Family Services. That voice held me steady when we found out one of our students was being prostituted and when we found out that another was homeless.

"Just keep teaching."

Adjusting Teaching and Learning

Whether you teach in an urban, suburban, or rural district, we are in this together because we largely serve the same system. And that system is racist, ableist, and one-size-fits-all. It is not nearly good enough, equitable enough, or even just enough for our babies.

You've seen the headlines. George Floyd. Ahmaud Arbery. Philando Castile. Breonna Taylor. Tamir Rice. Your own students. The stories that never make the evening news or the morning headlines. You have held the tears back just long enough to make it to the teacher's restroom before breaking down. The obituaries of ones that are so young that their favorite super-heroes are included in their funeral services. Gun violence or police violence that tears a mother away from her children and leaves a school community to pick up the pieces. The mourning and the crying give way to days of fear that grips with the reality that retaliation may strike at any time. And then, the protests, the words, but little change and less action.

Again, urban districts highlight issues that Black and Brown students face, but every district, every school is responsible for the larger culture and system that keeps those students down. We all have children who come to school for meals and who take a gamble and share details of their home life with those adults that they have deemed difference makers for their situation. Hopefully it is you! We bind up the brokenhearted and then try as best we can to explain to demanding community members the grades on a school report card, the ranking of districts on a list, or the performance of students on standardized tests.

We stand battle-tested and weary, yet committed! Research by Reardon, Robinson-Cimpian, & Weathers (2016) shows:

> Racial, ethnic, and socioeconomic disparities in academic achievement remain a stubborn feature of U.S. schooling. National studies consistently show that the average non-Hispanic Black student scores well below the average non-white student on standardized tests of math and reading skills, as does the average Hispanic student. Likewise, the average student from a low-income family scores much lower on such tests than students from higher-income families. Considerable attention has been focused on achievement gaps, particularly the Black-white achievement gap. Scholars and educators have suggested a number of possible explanations for the gaps, and policymakers, principals, and teachers have tried a range of remedies. . . . [T]he gaps persist despite these efforts. Moreover, our understanding of the causes and patterns of these achievement gaps is far from complete.

These facts are not to break educators down, but rather to build up an Honor Corps, with the force like that of the Marines, that takes these truths and builds learners that are equipped to beat the odds.

I have learned that education is the most rewarding recycling of heartbreak. There are plenty of circumstances that you could stare out of the window of your classroom and cry or you can decide that what we do in this classroom impacts what I see out there tomorrow.

Just teach.

UDL is a framework that reminds us why we teach. It is greater than content. It is greater than test scores. We teach because it is a calling to improve our cities and our world by believing the best about the students we serve.

Just keep teaching.

Helping Black and Brown Students Become Expert Learners

This does not mean that you ignore the circumstances. That would be impossible. Barriers to "just teaching" are many, including the punitive response to many so-called low performing districts—a chicken-and-egg dilemma that can leave educators fearing for the jobs or utilizing desperate measures to improve test scores quickly. The pressure to improve scores quickly even led one big-city superintendent to use illegal means to try to meet federal and state expectations (Fantz, 2015). She served time in prison, but the issue of commingled fear of failure and the reality of accountability have created schools that are operating in a culture steeped in consequence and punishment. Merit pay and teacher evaluations continue to be increasingly tied to student performance on one test. Teachers fear that failure is lurking just around every corner of innovation or improvement. Although the workforce demands critical thinking, problem-solving, teamwork and collaboration, communication skills, and a good work ethic, our education systems continue to emphasize student performance on tests (Gratz, 2009).

Still, the great teachers force the circumstances to serve our purposes. We can't stop teaching. We may close the books or darken the screens, but we never stop teaching. We never stop fighting. The truth is the real invitation has been given to us by the students we serve. Their potential is inviting us to stay focused beyond the distractions of real life—and just teach. As Beverly Daniel Tatum (2003) notes, impact—not intentions—are what matter when it comes to serving Black and Brown students. And for all the trying, our Black and Brown students are the ones most often left behind by these punitive regimes.

The goal for educators is to help students become expert learners. We have to make room for learners to struggle and use resources that they know to figure out problems that they don't know the answer to yet. Supported struggle (or challenge) means that learners are aware of the supports that are available to them and that they know how to use them in order to get through a complex text or task. Resourced struggle means that there are specific resources for the purpose of independently struggling through an academic task. Whether the supports are general or the resources are specific, the learner is able to make choices about how to genuinely find solutions, craft targeted questions, and identify the parts of the task that are causing a struggle. Learners become experts at examining whether they have enough information to make another move in their educational journey. Do we see our students as able to take control in their learning? Creating a learning environment that depends on the teacher dismisses the development of the muscle of struggling toward progress. Instead, we want students to become resourceful and knowledgeable learners, strategic and goal-directed learners, and purposeful and motivated learners—the definition of expert learners (Ertmer & Newby, 2006).

Picture your students upgrading their learning vehicles on the expressway to success with real-world problem solving and real-time resourcefulness. Imagine learners leveraging what they already know and relate to—great stores of wealth that can connect to academic content, such as home languages, family values and traditions, caregiving, friends and family, family outings, household chores, educational activities, favorite TV shows, family occupations and knowledge (National Center on Cultural and Linguistic Responsiveness, 2019).

Learning more about these areas empowers the learner as knowledgeable and having a positive contribution for the learning environment. There is honor and power when we invite the funds of knowledge that our learners and families have into their own learning experiences. In an antiracist, universally designed learning environment, the teacher learns about her students and families to discover the funds of knowledge to build bridges to content, experiences, school context and expectations to school and from school. Assuming that each student is rich with knowledge we will find many ways to connect to what they already know to unlock pathways to what they don't know.

We have to admit that learning can be scary if students are not equipped and prepared to become experts at learning. Hammond (2015) talks about the pitfalls of learners who must depend on the teacher to carry the cognitive load. She uses the term dependent learner to describe a learner who, on his own, "is not able to do complex, school-oriented learning tasks such as synthesizing and analyzing informational text without continuous support" (p.13).

If education is an expressway of learning, then some are traveling with the luxury of ease, and others who do not even have a way to the road. Students at a high risk of being left out, forgotten, and left as spectators on the side of the road benefit from the principles of Universal Design for Learning (UDL).

Virgil's story

In the next chapter, we will dive into the nuts and bolts of the UDL framework but first let's appreciate its power—the way you might enjoy seeing, smelling, and tasting a slice of pecan pie before you look at the recipe. The theoretical framework is critical for students to succeed, but first, we must dive into the real meaning of success—expert learning.

I am reminded of a young man named Virgil. He had an older brother who I had taught two years before. Our teaching team had raised concerns about Virgil because he was chronically absent. When he was present, he would be angry or combative. Trying a new approach to independent reading we asked students to select a book to read so they could learn more about how complex characters interact over the course of a text. We offered tools for students to personalize their journeys through the book of their choice.

Some students used a reading log to explore characters' actions, thoughts, and feelings, some used a recommendation form that they completed along the way, some used a storyboard cartoon sheet, some created paper dolls of the characters, and wrote quotes on the clothing. Virgil started with a reading log because it required the least amount of writing, but he quickly confessed that it was not helping him remember how and why the characters were changing. He walked around the room to see what other people were using and did an informal survey of how the tools helped the other students. He switched formats two or three times, but his announcement at the end of his book is what floored me. As we were hearing reviews of different books Virgil said, "I have never read a book from beginning to end before, until now. Usually, I read to take the test, or I just find what I need to find to do the project."

He found a method of learning to carry him from the beginning of the book to the end. His learning vehicle was a "hooptie," a junker at best. But because there was no assessment or project associated with this reading, he upgraded his vehicle to find pleasure in reading and identifying with complex characters with personal accountability. Virgil learned something about his own learning, and it could never be taken away from him.

Meyer, Rose, and Gordon (2014) note that, "Developing expertise in anything is always a process of continuous learning—practice, adjustment, and refinement. In the context of UDL, we focus on learning expertise: the lifelong process of becoming ever more motivated, knowledgeable, and skillful" (p. 21). Virgil took a step toward that lifelong process.

UDL provides a framework for every learner to get on the road to expert learner. He became what the Guidelines refer to as purposeful and motivated. Virgil found the motivation to pursue learning by reading. His own personal journey led him in pursuit of tools that work, versus methods that met an assignment's expectations. He tapped into a personal resilience that sustained his efforts. While working toward eliminating distractions, he was keenly aware of what worked for him, and what pulled him away from his goal of completing that book. Virgil's story teaches us the transforming power of learning environments that create and support expert learners.

Accessing the expressway of learning is a huge undertaking. Most times the expressway moves at a fast pace and gets people to their destinations more quickly than a roundabout street approach. While driving, I have seen rare times when the expressway was being utilized by more than just cars. I've seen walkers, motorcyclists, and bicyclists. Walkers and bikers usually stick to the shoulder. Being in the middle of the expressway would be a danger. Struggling learners trying to keep up on the education expressway need appropriate vehicles to stay safe and keep moving.

Dorian's story

Becoming an expert learner is the vehicle that makes learning safe and productive. Learning how to learn is what moves every student forward on this journey in a way that is meaningful and most enjoyable. The expressway of learning is a people mover, but educators have to make sure that we are preparing our students to drive the vehicle of their own learning in school, but more importantly in life.

I often think of a student I will call Dorian. There were many barriers keeping Dorian from success. He was a Black student in a system with institutional racism. He was affiliated with a gang and had a street reputation that preceded him into the school building. He was in the ninth grade but could not read. Would an end-of-course exam motivate Dorian to buckle down and get serious? Would the threat of the school moving into academic emergency be enough to get him to show up to interventions, where more drill-and-kill are promised? During a

coerced afterschool tutoring session, Dorian had willingly completed three timed fact sheets of 100 multiplication problems.
After his third set of 100, he had had enough. "No!" he stated
firmly. "I'm not doing another sheet! Not for practice! Not for
testing! Not for anything!" Multiplication was not his area of
need, but everyone was doing the same thing. Math first, then
a couple of reading passages with questions. Neither intervention met his need.

His refusal was met with punishment. Dorian didn't know
how to learn, and interventions were keeping him in a stalled
vehicle on the side of the road. He didn't know how to move forward, and he had grown tired of spinning his wheels in interventions that did not meet his needs or give him access to learning.
He was punished for being angry about having a stalled car on
the expressway of learning. Were others on the same road? Yes.
Were some moving ahead? Sure. Were there others stalled but
sitting quietly? Probably. But Dorian demanded a different kind
of roadside assistance by refusing to pretend that he was content in the parked position. He wanted to drive!

Are schools more readily offering the promise of learning
or the danger of failing for our brilliant Black and Brown students? We have to be mindful that traditional approaches to
education for some students, like Dorian, are danger zones,
not opportunity fields. This dangerous type of learning places
a student in the crosshairs of true failure because they give
a false sense of success. The eminent Spanish cellist, Pablo
Casals, once said:

> What do we teach our children? We teach them that two
> and two make four, and that Paris is the capital of France.
> When will we teach them what they *are*? You are a marvel.
> You are unique. In all the years that have passed, there has
> never been another child like you. You may become a Shake-
> speare, a Michelangelo, a Beethoven. You have the capacity
> for anything. Yes, you are a marvel.

Throughout this book, you will learn that UDL acknowledges the areas that need to be addressed—but through the lens of student's strengths and natural abilities and interests. Dorian could not read, but what an amazing artist he was. He had an eye for color and texture. He desperately wanted to use his art to share a message. That was our entry point. When students have not been equipped to merge onto the expressway of learning, then they are in the right place for action with the wrong mode of transportation. It's like being stalled on the side of the road, then starting up the vehicle only to roll over a strip of spikes. When they have discovered the inner marvel through learning, then their capacity to accelerate and excel expands right before our eyes.

The question is, "How do we help Dorian to merge with the gift that he has onto the expressway of learning to build up what he needs to get to his desired destination?" This is a complex question, but it is one that I believe the UDL Guidelines help us to ask and answer over and over again if we are committed to an antiracist lens.

UDL provides a framework for every member of the learning community to become an expert learner. Dorian has a gift for artistic renderings. He has a difficult time reading. Leveraging his strengths to attack the areas that will hinder his progress towards his goals means finding ways to empower him to be *resourceful and knowledgeable* while building his skills as a *strategic and goal-directed* learner.

Let's explore his situation through the lens of creating on-ramps to the expressway of success (Table 2.1). Imagine you want all students to grapple with complex text as they analyze a particular point of view or cultural experience reflected in a work of literature from outside the United States, drawing on a wide reading of world literature. You decide to help activate student background knowledge to help them to recognize the impact of Egyptian or Greek mythology on American literature. How can you ensure that all students, including Dorian, have

Table 2.1: On-ramps for Expert Learning

Resourceful and Knowledgeable	Strategic and Goal-Directed	UDL Strategies
Bring considerable prior knowledge to new learning.	Formulate plans for learning.	What do you know or what have you heard about Egyptian mythology and or Greek gods? Look at these images—architecture, hieroglyphics, the dollar bill, the post office emblem, Nike logo, Tennessee Titans, Trident, Venus. Look at the logos and the symbolism. What do you think they have to do with Egyptian culture or Greek gods?
Activate that prior knowledge to identify, organize, prioritize, and assimilate new information.	Devise effective strategies and tactics to optimize learning.	Read about Egyptian and Greek mythologies online or in a book. Use the TSS reader or read on your own to find out what inspired each company from Greek mythology. Can you see any similarities between the Greek gods and Egyptian gods? Create and record a pretend dialogue between the Greeks to the new companies. You can use a chart or Venn Diagram.

Table 2.1: (*Continued*)

Resourceful and Knowledgeable	Strategic and Goal-Directed	UDL Strategies
		You can create a song that exposes the secrets behind the logos.
		Draw a storyboard that shows how each company got inspired by mythology. Try to show the moment of imagined inspiration.
		Read a few articles about the assertion that Greeks got their ideas from Egyptians. Form your own opinion and create a blog or a series of tweets that tell the truth about each logo or the connection between the two civilizations.
		If you have another idea to organize this information, please discuss it with me before moving forward.
Recognize the tools and resources that would help learners find, structure, and remember new information.	Organize resources and tools to facilitate learning.	Have each tool hyperlinked to the assignment.
		Make it available in print, video, or audio recording so that students will be able to choose what works best.

Continued on the next page

Table 2.1: (*Continued*)

Resourceful and Knowledgeable	Strategic and Goal-Directed	UDL Strategies
Know how to transform new information into meaningful and useful knowledge.	Monitor their progress:	Reflect on the learning: Record a video, write a blog post, or draw a picture that answers the following questions: *Before I read this article I was familiar with the meaning of _____. After reading the article I was surprised to learn _____. Based on what I have read in this article, I expect this story,* The Odyssey, *to be about _____?* Set up an online account with Trello or another tool to break any project into small tasks. Provide supports such as conferencing, check-ins, virtual and peer feedback.
Teach self-reflection	Students recognize their own strengths and weaknesses as learners.	Quick conference: Tell me why you chose the options you did? What would you have chosen if those options were not available? Tell me why?

Table 2.1: (*Continued*)

Resourceful and Knowledgeable	Strategic and Goal-Directed	UDL Strategies
		Which option would you like to choose next time? What can you do between now and then to be better prepared for another option? When will you work toward this goal? What help do you need to get there?

authentic, meaningful experiences to build knowledge, make choices about their learning, connect with rigorous text, and share their strengths even if they haven't built functional literacy skills? The answer: Find on-ramps.

Dorian used his art skills to draw pictures and illustrate the plot of the stories he listened to from our literature book. He found a way to chronicle the changes in the characters and explicate his understanding to others. He was resistant to outside tutoring but committed to engaging with the literature. He made text-to-self connections, particularly with *The Odyssey*. There were times during class when Dorian would forget he had on his headphones and he would jump out of his seat cheering for the hero of the epic poem.

One day he left a note for me on my desk. It said, "I am god. I am death." I hadn't opened it until he left the room, so I didn't have the benefit of conversing with him about the cryptic message. I took the note to the principal and asked her to have a joint conversation with both of us. She called him into her office without me and questioned him about the note.

He stormed straight into my classroom yelling, "Why did you give that to her. I drew that for you!"

I lowered my voice just above a whisper, "Dorian, do you know what that paper said?"

He shook his head no and lowered his eyes.

I told him the context of his note and asked him where he had gotten those words.

"I copied them from the newspaper. I thought you would be happy that I got something from the newspaper." He had recognized some of the letters and wanted to make words—for me. He just happened to copy the card from a report about the infamous DC sniper attacks in 2002, and his message got a bit mixed up.

Dorian exhibited a love for art coupled with a desire to read. He began meeting with a tutor, but only after finding ways to conceal their meeting. When they met during the time he was scheduled in my class, he convinced his buddies he was skipping. He met with the tutor nonetheless. Through it all he exercised a tenacity and a love for learning. The stereotypes don't account for a young Black male who wants to learn. Dorian was interested in literature and art. He had the capacity and the capability to enjoy, analyze, and interpret complex texts. He didn't have access until he found an avenue.

Carol Dweck, a leader in the field of motivation, personality, and developmental psychology, shared some insight into Dorian's kind of mindset in an interview with *Education World*:

> There is *no* relation between students' abilities or intelligence and the development of mastery-oriented qualities. Some of the very brightest students avoid challenges, dislike effort, and wilt in the face of difficulty. And some of the less bright students are real go-getters, thriving on challenge, persisting intensely when things get difficult, and accomplishing more than you expected. This is something

that really intrigued me from the beginning. It shows that being mastery-oriented is about having the right mind-set. It is not about how smart you are. However, having the mastery-oriented mind-set will help students become more able over time (Hopkins, 2015).

Dorian never wanted to communicate the wrong message again, so he decided to learn to read, no matter what. When things got difficult or he got frustrated he would take himself for a walk and return to work. He transferred in the middle of his sophomore year, but he had developed a mindset and learning skillset to get him to the next level. With training and tenacity, he fought through his barriers and made use of the options made available to him. He had choices that became on-ramps for him to the expressway of learning. He became his own advocate, exhibiting a self-advocacy that revved up with just a push start. Dorian had options to read, discuss and analyze the Odyssey. He had options to choose another text that meets the same standards. Black and Brown children deserve access to rigorous texts and powerful learning experiences that build their own personal learning as a vehicle to success. That is the power of Universal Design for Learning. That is the power of antiracist learning environments.

Reflection

In their book *Best Practice: Bringing Standards to Life in America's Classrooms*, Zemelman, Daniels, & Hyde (2012) suggest some practices to decrease and some to increase in the classroom. These include but are not limited to:

- Less whole-class, teacher-directed instruction

- Less solitude and working alone

- Less rigidity in classroom seating arrangements
- Less time spent reading textbooks and basal readers
- Fewer pull-out special programs
- More active learning, with all the attendant noise and movement of students doing and talking
- More flexible seating and working areas in the classroom
- More diverse roles for teachers, including coaching, demonstrating, and modeling
- More reading of real texts: whole books, primary sources, and nonfiction materials
- More heterogeneous classrooms where individual needs are met through individualized activities not segregation of bodies.
- More reliance on descriptive evaluations of student growth, including observational/ anecdotal records, conference notes, and performance assessment rubrics (pp. 6-7)

3

Safety Checks on the UDL Expressway

UDL and antiracism converge to form an expressway to success. Everyone knows you don't get behind the wheel the first time and head off to the expressway unaccompanied, right? It is the same with the implementation of UDL when serving our Black and Brown students. While implementation takes training and practice, there are some additional factors that will create the right environment for this shift in teaching and learning to take place.

Before we rev up those engines, we need to check the mirrors, put on our seat belts, adjust the seats and the steering wheel. Let's check a few safety tips.

Check 1: Antiracism

The work of antiracism is active, not passive. Antiracists are not born, nor can a teacher be made an antiracist. Each individual must choose to actively recognize racist barriers and do the work to tear them down. In our classrooms and educational systems there many areas to evaluate our actions to challenge ourselves to ensure we are doing the work of an antiracist. There is no fully comprehensive list but antiracist educators are committed to a lifetime of pursuing education that informs their actions to dismantle racist systems.

As we dig into this work, know that there is nothing that exempts any teacher from operating from a racist mindset. Because systems are set up to favor whiteness and white privilege—it is possible for Black and Brown teachers to utilize racist practices in our classrooms. We have to challenge our notion of "rightness." What makes a solution right? What makes a way of speaking right? What makes the way that we access a text right? Often rightness has equated to whiteness— which excludes the genius of Black and Brown students simply because they have different methods. Different is *not* a deficit, but in racist systems the penalty can be exclusion, suspension, identified as special education and an overall message of not being willing or able to achieve.

Here are a few questions to consider as you evaluate your teaching to see if where you need to take more antiracist actions. In 2020, the African American Student Union at the Harvard Graduate School of Design issued a list of action steps to address the institutionalized racism they faced as students there (Budds, 2020). From their list, I adapted some ideas for educators in every school system to think through and truly examine where we are in these areas as a catalyst or continuation of antiracist work.

1. Are Black and Brown voices reflected in the curricula and/ or curricula resources?

2. Are there Black and Brown people teaching Black and Brown students? This is not only an issue for human resources to figure out but one for antiracist teachers to press no matter where they are.

3. Has there been a concerted effort to have continuing self-reflective conversations about antiracist practices?

4. Are we acknowledging the work of promoting justice in meaningful ways within the system?

5. Do we include speakers who model academic excellence and attainment for Black or Brown learners?

6. Does the system value and protect those who speak out against racism, racist jokes, comments or a dichotomous experience that is different for Black and Brown students and their white counterparts?

7. Are Black and Brown students receiving honors and academic accolades?

8. Does every student have access to the tools, resources, and supports for success in your class and in your school system? How do you know? What will you do to find out?

9. Is there a real connection to the community? Are Black and Brown people welcome in your school or school system? Has there been a concerted effort to gain insight from Black and Brown people to design your curricula, systems, supports, or resources?

Answering these questions will show each practitioner whether we are glorifying whiteness by excluding Black and Brown voices from our learning design. It will lead us to reconsider at how we punish, ridicule, and praise. We have to examine who has the power if we are serious about distributing it. We have to be honest about racist ideologies that have masqueraded as policies, rules, and traditions for decades. Antiracist are committed to self-examination and system examination to ensure that not one hint of the racism is left untouched.

Check 2: Reducing Student Stress

Students come to school and bring with them a myriad of concerns. Students are highly stressed about many things. Universally designed classrooms can reduce stress by building trust and providing options. Trust in a classroom setting means that all stakeholders know the expectations. There are very few surprises when it comes to rituals and routines. I know what to expect from you and you know what to expect from me. This does not mean that we do exactly the same thing each day. It simply means that I have a mental framework for how things are done, expectations, and consequences.

Trust is essential in all learning environments but particularly in urban classrooms. Reducing stress with trust is the foundational building block to a dynamic learning environment. According to a report by the Urban Education Network (2017),

> Research has shown that over 80 percent of inner-city youth experience one or more traumatic events in their lives. Neurobiological research tells us that such repeated stress causes brain and hormonal changes; it repeatedly puts students in fight-or-flight states that can impede the development of skills needed for healthy interpersonal relations, concentration, and learning " (p.2).

With the high probability of trauma, learning environments have to be transformed on a foundation of trust.

Building trust is difficult. As Aguilar (2017) notes, "Whether in a conversation or during a class, whoever intends to build trust (the teacher, coach, principal) needs to have five positive or neutral interactions with another person for every one corrective piece of feedback. That's what it takes to build and maintain trust." Think of ways to build in positive or neutral feedback for each student. Perhaps it is the greeting at the door, affirmation activities, or goal conferencing. How do you intend to build trust to decrease stress? Decreasing stress and building trust lead to community.

UDL depends greatly on learning community buy-in. Students will have the freedom to make choices about their learning and options for their assessments. For the community buy-in to be sincere, students need to know that their work time will be protected and free from unnecessary distractions. If a guest speaker is brought in, that event should flow with the expected schedule of work time, not interrupt it. Also, make sure that distractions are minimized and that learning spaces are varied to encourage choices in workspaces. Make sure that when community property is used that it is cared for and placed in the right location at the end of the class. This is not just the teacher's responsibility, but the community of learners' responsibility. There are many dangers to a learning community's time and space. Make a list of scenarios and come up with solutions or preventive efforts that the community can take to make sure the classroom is protected and productive at all times.

Check 3: The Power of Listening

Communication skills are essential life skills. Giving students the space and freedom to listen and view content while forming an opinion is critically important to life success. Listening to and conversing with someone you disagree with is rare in today's society. Using protocols for how to give and receive feedback will empower students to interject their voices into conversations in a variety of formats and media. Students will be able to practice this skill to prepare for real world interactions. Protocols even the playing field for students who are used to sharing their thoughts and feelings openly to others who don't share very much and even still others have the opportunity to learn how to reject a claim without rejecting the claimant. Having protocols helps the community to feel safe and to learn how to interact respectfully. Protocols won't be necessary for everyone all year long, but they will help the community of learners communicate respectfully, thus reducing stress and making it a safe place to share and receive feedback. Try a protocol like this to walk students through the expectations for listening.

Reflection

Four Simple Steps for Listening Safely

1. Protect Your Head. Direct your thoughts toward the speaker/video. Letting your mind drift can be dangerous to your goal of listening to learn. How can you personalize your environment to give you the best space for keeping your thoughts engaged?

2. Obey All Traffic Lights and Laws. Interacting with the speaker means you STOP doing anything else. Use CAUTION when making any noise that will take away from the speaker or other listeners. GO with the speaker by responding appropriately to their material. Others in the classroom may use the clues that they interpret to change the light on their desk. If you need visual clues, look around near you.

3. Look Out for Other Listeners. If you know you are next to listeners who may use a method to engage with the learning that is distracting to you feel free to move your seat before the presentation begins. Do whatever it takes for you to stay focused and listen safely to the speaker. Don't weave in and out of attentiveness. Try not to participate in any distracting behavior.

4. Use Your Signals. Eye contact, head nodding, and taking notes are all ways to SIGNAL to the speaker that you are listening. Let them know you are with them throughout the speech.

Note: The learning community will personalize the protocol to fit the needs of the group.

Check 4: Behavioral Expectations

Anytime a group comes together there are many different definitions for what's acceptable. Some families are loud and talk over each other. Some families don't express personal views at all. Still others are highly confrontational or sensitive. Other families tease and poke fun at each other without taking offense at all. And some people may blur the lines between all different styles. No matter where the members of a group are from, one thing is for sure, we all come to the table with different definitions of normal and acceptable.

Part of the UDL experience is to prepare for all kinds of students ahead of time. Plan to gather input on behavioral expectations in a variety of ways. Have students text suggestions for classroom expectations or share a story about what could go wrong without the expectations. You may want to offer a suggestion box or an exit ticket to garner input. Allow the community of learners to shape the expectations for this group. Also, decide how the group will hold themselves accountable to these expectations. Plan upfront to define success and plan a celebration if the goals are met. Positive intent with behavioral norms removes the threat of negativity and sets up a growth mindset to achieve what we attempt.

In a blog post, special educator and PBIS coach Dustin Bindreiff (2016) offers this powerful insight:

> Teachers who bring a growth mindset to interpreting a child's problem behavior are likely to adopt more of an instructional approach to behavior. Teachers in a growth mindset are likely to see problem behaviors as skill deficits, not person deficits. With this understanding they will develop a plan to help the child acquire new skills to express him or herself in more socially appropriate ways.

Bindreiff notes that so-called "defiant" students are often telling teachers "I'm not ready to work right now." Educators with a growth mindset will understand this and find ways to help students communicate in socially appropriate ways, he notes. Educators with a fixed mindset jump focus on curbing the behavior rather than understanding and responding to its underlying causes. "Doing so," writes Bindreiff, "creates two potentially problematic strategies: 'getting tough' so the student doesn't get away with it or avoiding situations that may cause the child to misbehave. If instead, a growth mindset is adopted, the teacher is more likely to focus on teaching the skills the child needs so that she can express herself in a more socially appropriate way."

Safety is much more than just the threat of physical harm. Just as we discussed norms for behavior, it is equally important to make sure that acceptable behaviors and speech are defined within the learning community. Sure, we do this at the beginning of the year and then check the activity off as done. For a UDL classroom to succeed, it has to be a place where students are free to take risks, ask questions, and be honored for being themselves.

To keep an environment of freedom, there needs to be frequent reminders and refreshers. Remind students of acceptable behaviors. Plan in advance for groups to remind the class through their choice of a song, or a video or a poster or a blog post of what is expected behavior and how our community deals with inappropriate behaviors and how we celebrate expected behavior. Are the behavioral expectations both clear and clearly supported to help students engage in expected behavior? Are the expectations refreshing to the learning environment or restrictive?

Check 5: Setting Goals, Solving Problems

It's not enough for someone to tell me what I've done wrong. I need to understand the expectations and then build a plan for working through the scenario so that I can reach my personal goal of being an outstanding community member, an avid contributor, and an expert learner. Consequently, a community of learners does not grow by only reflecting on the unmet expectations. Walk your learners through the process of setting community goals, celebrating the goals they meet, providing community support for those who are struggling, and setting more challenging and rigorous goals once we repeatedly reach our benchmark. One activity that helps to set the tone for community and teamwork is Circle Maker.

Try It!

Circle Maker

- The purpose of this activity is to transform a random group into a learning community.

- Ask everyone to have a seat at their desk or table. After you have the group's attention, simply give this direction with no explanation: Move the desks or tables into a circle and when you are done have a seat.

- Secretly use a stopwatch to record how long it takes to get everyone to move. Silently observe the transition and do not offer any guidance at all. When all the desks and/or tables are in a circle and each person is seated, stop the timer. Write the time on the board for the entire class to see.

- Announce the time to the class—"It took 7 minutes and 47 seconds to move the tables into a circle"—and have all students seated.

- Guide the class through a series of reflection questions:

  o Why do you think it took that long? List the responses on the board. Try to hear from everyone.

  o Who gave helpful input to accomplish the task?

o Do you think that 7 minutes and 47 seconds is a time that we can beat as a learning community?

o How will we do that?

• Record the plan on the board and review it.

• Put the desk or chairs back in their original positions and when everyone is seated and ready, give them the direction and time them again. Cross out the old time and write the new time up on the board.

• Ask the class: Why was this time different?

This is our plan every time we transition from groups to a circle. This is our game plan for every assignment. We will use our experiences to figure out a new path. We will rely on the community to make each individual stronger. We will make a plan to lead to success. We will listen when appropriate. We will lead when necessary. We will make every second count. If we do that, we will succeed.

Have them try the activity one last time to see if they can beat the improved time. The group will learn that the strategies and solutions that they come up with for themselves are much more powerful than an outside force. Problem solving is a muscle that every learner has to build for success.

Check 6: Moving Past Fear and Bias

Because safety is important, every teacher has to reflect in the rearview mirror of their past experiences, fears, biases, and expectations. Are you fearful of the students, or the area, or the tasks, or what you see on the news? Be honest with yourself and dig deeply into what you are afraid of.

Talk to a colleague about which fears are reasonable and which ones are not. Business writer Michael Hyatt describes reframing your fear as turning "what's otherwise debilitating into something motivating." Reframing your fear will model resilience for your students in ways that may never even reach the surface of the conversation but will shine through in your resolve.

Urban teaching is not for the faint at heart and truth be told there are many dangers, but what overrides that foreboding sense of what could happen to you, is what could happen through you. The fear is real, but so is the possibility of changing the quality of life for a student who receives a key to unlock learning for the rest of their life.

Coming to terms with our biases and expectations is one of hardest things to deal with:

What are the thoughts you have when you hear that a new student is coming to you and has an IEP?

Do you automatically think about how to dial down the rigor, instead of thinking of various ways to communicate the standard clearly?

What do you expect from children of various races and ethnicities?

Do you stereotype different groups of students based on what you think they are like, or what you think they will like?

Are you willing to examine the pronouns you use to address a child who may be gender neutral?

If you have no clue what that is, are you willing to keep learning in order to lead the classroom environment as a safe zone free of bullying and bias?

Are you willing to ask yourself some deep and possibly even disturbing questions to minimize barriers to learning for every student from every walk of life that sets foot in your classroom, no matter what?

Are you willing to discuss how you see, and design for, and fight the system to ensure positive outcomes for your Black and Brown students?

Are you willing to make your classroom safe, and then push every known entity in the school and the district to become safe as well?

I'm willing to stir up a little trouble to keep our kids safe! We owe it to our students to create safe undisturbed domiciles of learning that force the troubles of this world into submission. Creating resilience in our students allows them to develop and grow into agents of change, first in the classroom and then out in the real world. Driving change to occur all around them begins with feeling safe to try. While we are not exempt from what is happening in the streets around us, we are examples of how to navigate the streets and survive. Emotionally, physically, and mentally safe classrooms will lead to optimal student achievement in partnership with the teacher.

Keeping learners safe compels us to examine any barriers the learners bring with them to the classroom. Two decades of research by psychologists Claude Steele, Joshua Aronson, and Steven Spencer has shown the power of stereotype threat to impact performance in the classroom and on standardized tests. In short, when students are aware of the stereotypes about them—that they can't perform up to high standards—the doubt and self-pressure they feel actually suppresses their performance. It's like a self-fulfilling prophecy. Stereotype threat negatively impacts the performance and the barrier of perception becomes actualized. This is dangerous for learners and makes conditions unsafe for their progress and performance on tests that are gatekeepers for access to various roads.

In safe classrooms we are always teaching. We have to be aware of the messages we send and the messages the learners come to us believing. Seat belts are on. Mirrors are adjusted. Safe to "Just Teach."

Reflection

- Am I committed to learning and growing so that my students can learn and grow?

- Have I been fretting about the problem while losing valuable time to change the world through rigorous relevant creative instruction?

- Are my students yielding to my preconceived notions about their neighborhood and circumstances?

- Am I ready to disturb the peace of those for whom chaos is a normality?

Building the UDL Expressway

Educators of Black and Brown students will be reminded of the impossibility, discouraged by the difficulty, chastised with the reality but rewarded with the opportunity to make dreams come true one student at a time. Academic success for all is a lofty idea, but "all" takes a strong, dedicated group of enlightened ones and a framework designed to eliminate inequities. With Universal Design for Learning, we can embrace our ability to honor our students and provide on-ramps for all of our students so they can experience driving toward their own definition of success. But creating world changers isn't just busy work or the kind of work that traditional schools are used to. The work of a revolutionary antiracist—ignited by the need for change and the body of research that points to what is possible—is burning hot with the passion to reach all students.

UDL offers a framework for customizing goals, methods, materials, and assessments that showcase the brilliance of every student, not just one "type" of learner (Meyer, Rose, & Gordon, 2014; Novak, 2016). This construct is not an educational silver bullet meant to fix all problems, but rather a flexible, customizable way to help us teach students to become expert learners. One-size-fits-all education creates barriers that block the brilliance of many learners—and too often the brilliance of our Black and Brown students.

A teacher shared with me a time when her frustration was tangible. She had given very clear directions for everyone to complete a worksheet that reinforced the distributive property. She walked over to a young man who had slid down as far as he possibly could on the desk without capsizing like a canoe on a river. She barely parted her lips as she scolded him three times—each with more heated intensity, "Sit up. Sit UP. SIT UP NOW!"

She recalled how this scene played out dozens of times before she offered options for silent work time. Now learners can choose to work silently at a standing desk, in a bean bag, or on a rug. Her silent work time is given in 10-minute chunks instead of full class periods. "I'm amazed at how much this has changed our dynamic in the classroom," she says. "Just a few options gave unlimited learning freedom not only to that young man, but so many others."

UDL begins by recognizing, simply, that all students are capable of learning and really want to learn. Our instructional design prevents them from doing so. Our students come to us with a unique mix of strengths and weaknesses and we are called to create an environment that eliminates the barriers that would prevent success, even when they are present at a systems level. When our students are not successful, the first place we should look for an explanation is the curriculum, not the learner. What is getting in the way?

Traditional systems that perpetuate institutional racism and block on-ramps to learning are designed for a mythical average learner, one who is white, privileged, at grade-level, and self-regulated. The default language, culture, social and economic assumptions, and goals of traditional public education are oriented toward the white, suburban middle class. Often educators will say that our systems are broken. This is not true. Our systems are doing exactly what they were designed to do—allow white privileged students to succeed and move ahead while others are held back. UDL requires us to do better—to name the barriers, like racism, and eliminate them by providing while maintaining high achievement standards for all.

To eliminate barriers, UDL empowers all learners by providing multiple means of engagement, multiple means of representation, and multiple means of action and expression. This means that learners will have more ways to interact with content, more ways to personalize paths to a learning goal, and more ways to evaluate the power of their learning (Rose & Gravel, 2009). The UDL approach scientifically customizes the route of learning, much in the way a GPS device finds the best approach to a destination, and reduces barriers and obstacles. UDL leverages and builds on the strengths of the learner to empower and embolden them.

UDL is focused on activating three networks of the brain that are responsible for learning: the affective network, the recognition network, and the strategic network (Rose & Meyer, 2002).

- **The Affective Network** is responsible for motivating students and recruiting their interest. Without activating this network, students will not see the purpose of learning.

- **The Recognition Network** translates information and turns it into something meaningful to build comprehension. The Recognition Network allows a student to understand and make sense of information.

- **The Strategic Network** must be activated for students to use the information they learned. It allows students to express what they have learned in valuable and useful ways.

The three principles of UDL support educators in creating multiple pathways for students to learn and express what they know while empowering students to make choices about their learning (Meyer, Rose, & Gordon, 2014).

Provide multiple means of engagement: Engagement is at the core of all learning experiences. If we want students to learn, we have to foster both attention and commitment by providing students with authentic, meaningful experiences in learning that are culturally responsive and antiracist.

Provide multiple means of representation: The second principle of UDL reminds educators to provide multiple means of representation to build knowledge and comprehension in all learners. There must be multiple access and entry points so all students can grow as learners as they reach toward the same goal.

Provide multiple means of action and expression: Students need numerous methods to express their understanding as they develop into writers and speakers. Traditionally, students were asked to share their understanding using one only means of action. When teachers provide students with multiple options, learners can choose the best option to demonstrate that they met the goal.

The UDL Guidelines (Fig. 4.1) are an essential tool for implementation. Still, this implementation can be like learning to walk a tightrope. You can learn all the theories and techniques, but until you actually step on that wire, you'll never know the risk—or excitement—of actually doing it. Whether the tight rope is two inches off the floor or two feet or two stories, each step involves risk. As Vygotsky (1978) points out in the concept of the zone of proximal development, there must be scaffolding and support. When there is a strong balance of support and challenge, there is a safety net to try and learn and reflect and start the cycle all over again.

Commit to your UDL journey with your colleagues. Where there is support, challenge, and feedback, there will be risk and growth. When teachers and leaders are a part of a community that encourages the risk with an understanding of the reward there will be managed innovation and exciting rewards. Where

The Universal Design for Learning Guidelines

CAST | Until learning has no limits

Provide multiple means of Engagement

Affective Networks
The "WHY" of Learning

Provide multiple means of Representation

Recognition Networks
The "WHAT" of Learning

Provide multiple means of Action & Expression

Strategic Networks
The "HOW" of Learning

Provide options for
Recruiting Interest (7)
- Optimize individual choice and autonomy (7.1)
- Optimize relevance, value, and authenticity (7.2)
- Minimize threats and distractions (7.3)

Provide options for
Perception (1)
- Offer ways of customizing the display of information (1.1)
- Offer alternatives for auditory information (1.2)
- Offer alternatives for visual information (1.3)

Provide options for
Physical Action (4)
- Vary the methods for response and navigation (4.1)
- Optimize access to tools and assistive technologies (4.2)

Provide options for
Sustaining Effort & Persistence (8)
- Heighten salience of goals and objectives (8.1)
- Vary demands and resources to optimize challenge (8.2)
- Foster collaboration and community (8.3)
- Increase mastery-oriented feedback (8.4)

Provide options for
Language & Symbols (2)
- Clarify vocabulary and symbols (2.1)
- Clarify syntax and structure (2.2)
- Support decoding of text, mathematical notation, and symbols (2.3)
- Promote understanding across languages (2.4)
- Illustrate through multiple media (2.5)

Provide options for
Expression & Communication (5)
- Use multiple media for communication (5.1)
- Use multiple tools for construction and composition (5.2)
- Build fluencies with graduated levels of support for practice and performance (5.3)

Provide options for
Self Regulation (9)
- Promote expectations and beliefs that optimize motivation (9.1)
- Facilitate personal coping skills and strategies (9.2)
- Develop self-assessment and reflection (9.3)

Provide options for
Comprehension (3)
- Activate or supply background knowledge (3.1)
- Highlight patterns, critical features, big ideas, and relationships (3.2)
- Guide information processing and visualization (3.3)
- Maximize transfer and generalization (3.4)

Provide options for
Executive Functions (6)
- Guide appropriate goal-setting (6.1)
- Support planning and strategy development (6.2)
- Facilitate managing information and resources (6.3)
- Enhance capacity for monitoring progress (6.4)

Access

Build

Internalize

Goal

Expert learners who are...

Purposeful & Motivated

Resourceful & Knowledgeable

Strategic & Goal-Directed

udlguidelines.cast.org | © CAST, Inc. 2018 | Suggested Citation: CAST (2018). Universal design for learning guidelines version 2.2 [graphic organizer]. Wakefield, MA: Author.

Figure 4.1: The UDL Guidelines

the tight rope was once daunting, it is now a welcomed challenge! Though it never gets easy, the walker just becomes more prepared. And that is when the walker becomes worth watching and the dream is sparked in a watcher that can also become a walker in the right conditions.

Multiple Avenues to Learning Goals

I've noticed while driving that when there is construction on the road, sometimes there are potholes that would damage a vehicle. In an order to make sure that drivers and their vehicles are safe, construction crews lay a metal plate over the obstruction and place signage to alert the driver that a plate is there to shield them from the danger. While it is true that some cars could make it over the obstruction with no damage at all, others would become inoperable if they met with what was beneath the metal plate.

These "potholes" are harmless to some but detrimental to others, so every teacher of Black and Brown students must evaluate the road to learning for the students they serve. Ignoring the potholes means ignoring the danger that some students are in. Acknowledging the potholes means that we prepare in advance for every learner no matter the condition of their learning vehicle.

Sometimes implementing UDL in combination with other frameworks can minimize the danger of "potholes" and provide additional protections for learners. Imagine UDL as the smooth paved road and the metal plate as a connector with UDL to make sure every learner travels with minimal disruption on their way. For example, UDL informed by Culturally Responsive Teaching covers the pothole of ignoring cultural differences. UDL informed by Trauma Responsive Teaching covers the pothole of ignoring the impact of trauma on the ability to learn. UDL informed by Social Emotional Learning covers the pothole of subtracting the human factor from the learner's profile.

UDL and Other Change Initiatives

One constant in education is change. In the last 20 years I have seen initiatives come and go. Sometimes an old pot of money is depleted, and a new pot is introduced with different strings attached. Other times the standards change, and therefore everything must change with it. We have to change to survive.

One of the reasons that I have held on so tightly to the Universal Design for Learning framework is because it has been so steadfast. UDL has been a constant through No Child Left Behind, the Every Student Succeeds Act, three adoptions of state standards, new assessments, Race to the Top, and federal funding formulas associated with School Improvement Grants. Locally we were able to keep in place despite changes in curricula, programs, structures, superintendents, and millions of other variables. I had to take several deep breaths after listing those changes. I lived through them all, but change is real and unnerving.

Finding a framework that holds its teeth in the face of change yet fits the requirement of the day is refreshing and empowering. UDL does just that. It gives school personnel a way to grab a hold to something they have the freedom to refine and define. This is something that can be introduced without the fear of it being removed or replaced with the next flavor of school improvement. No matter what the focus becomes for the federal government, the state departments of education or the local community—Universal Design for Learning will always fit and always make sense. We have to adapt and design to meet the needs of the learners we serve.

To show examples of how UDL can inform and be informed by other frameworks, I have examined some common school improvement foci and highlighted a few linkages between the frameworks or models. Start thinking of the initiatives in your district or building and see what similarities you can find with UDL.

UDL and Restorative Justice

Restorative Justice is a set of practices that helps educational systems move away from the zero tolerance policies that so often negatively impact Black and Brown students. Instead of zero tolerance restorative justice recognizes when an expectation has been broken but seeks a path to help learners reflect on their decisions and how those decisions impact the learning community. This reflection helps to restore the learner not stigmatize, punish, and exclude the learner.

At the core of restorative practices is a deeply embedded communal aspect. Universal Design for Learning promotes individual aspects, but not at the expense of the learning community. UDL points to the power of fostering collaboration and community to cultivate a community of learners. Fostering community is built in the restorative justice model by voluntary participation and respect for everyone involved. UDL also optimizes individual choice and autonomy to build engagement.

Every opportunity for dialogue must also embody those principles. By embodying these principles threats and distractions are minimized. The goal of the restorative practices is to expand the capacity of the community to create a fair and just response. A universally designed learning environment invites and protects every member of the community, by recognizing each member of the learning community as both valuable and redeemable regardless of their actions.

UDL and Culturally Responsive Teaching

In an interview with *Education Week*, Zaretta Hammond describes Culturally Responsive Teaching as a way to help "culturally and linguistically diverse students who have been marginalized in schools build their skill and capacity to do rigorous work. The focus isn't on motivation but on improving their brainpower and information processing skills" (Ferlazzo, 2015).

While Culturally Responsive Teaching can never be boiled down to a nice neat set of strategies, it is a mindset that fits with Universal Design for Learning to reach learners who are traditionally not thought of when planning instruction. In her book *Culturally Responsive Teaching and the Brain*, Hammond (2014) introduces a Warm Demander Chart. This chart encourages "active demandingness" with personal warmth, one which has high expectations for students, recognizes and encourages their abilities, and helps them reach their goals.

Some of the checkpoints in the UDL Guidelines sound very close to the warm demander characteristics. The ones that are the heating elements of a warm demander are found in multiple means of action and expression where students have options for appropriate goal setting and support for planning and strategy development.

What is best for culturally and linguistically diverse students is encompassed in what is best for all students who are at risk of being marginalized and excluded by the curriculum. UDL and Culturally Responsive Teaching are both based on brain research that invites all learners to the table with tools and strategies that encourage empowerment through choice and agency. Making sure that all learners have access to rigorous outcomes is the goal of both UDL and Culturally Responsive Teaching.

There is no such thing as a learning environment that is truly universally designed and not culturally responsive. Also, there is no way to be truly culturally responsive without universally designing the learning experiences. Ignoring culture creates a pothole that will both damage and deter some students. Being intentional about being culturally responsive in a universally designed environment puts the metal plate of safety on the road for all learners.

UDL and Trauma-Informed Practice

Trauma in students is often invisible. We can't look at a student and see that they stayed at home alone last night. We can't see that the primary giver is their grandmother, and she has been behaving erratically because she doesn't have access to her normal regimen of medication. Many times, trauma is not only invisible but is kept as a closely guarded secret. Very rarely have I had students self report traumatic incidents simply because the events or experiences are normalized in their households. This is not blaming the home or the parents, it is stating that there are times when Trauma can bubble below the surface, and only the student's behaviors or symptoms give hints to educators that something is amiss.

Trauma is often connected to adverse childhood experiences, or ACEs. ACEs, are potentially traumatic events that occur in childhood (0-17 years) such as experiencing violence, abuse, or neglect; witnessing violence in the home; and having a family member attempt or die by suicide. The Centers for Disease Control identifies 10 ACEs to look for (Joining Forces for Children, 2020):

Physical abuse,	incarcerated relative,
physical neglect,	sexual abuse,
emotional abuse,	mental illness,
emotional neglect,	substance abuse,
mother treated violently,	and divorce.

Research suggests that Black and Brown students are at greater risk for having experienced four or more of these ACEs. It's clear, then, that UDL practitioners must be trauma informed.

We may never know what is happening, but if we think ahead about trauma and structure our classrooms in a way that creates safety zones for students who may be experiencing traumatic events, we cover a pothole that may have otherwise dented and damaged an already traumatized learner. Students who are experiencing trauma or who are traumatized by a past event can internalize guilt, pain, and shame.

In her book, *Finding Your Best Self: Recovery from Addiction, Trauma, or Both,* Lisa Najavits (2019) says that one way to cope from trauma is creativity. She writes: "Creativity allows you to convert emotional pain into authentic expressions of your truth that inspire others or contribute to the world. Creativity can occur through traditional arts such as painting, writing, and theater; and broadly, through intellectual work, spiritual pursuit, or a social justice mission" (p. 40).

The connection with trauma-informed and trauma-responsive practices can be found throughout the Guidelines but particularly in providing multiple means of engagement by facilitating personal coping skills and strategies. Providing options for self regulation could include offering drawing, writing, and creating graphics as a way to engage with content. By connecting this understanding to the trauma informed methodology, the options for how to engage with their school work could be facilitating personal healing that goes far beyond the goal of the topic. Giving students choices empowers them and offers protection from the adverse consequences of trauma.

Providing multiple means of action and expression also can help educators address trauma. Using varied media for communication, construction, and composition, and building fluencies with graduated levels of support for practice and performance gives the learner a chance to try different avenues to express themselves to the learning community and beyond.

The universally designed classroom gives space for healing and coping. The student can be as vocal or as private about trauma as they choose. The Guidelines are steeped in empowerment which gives all students an opportunity to practice in safety and present their learning in confidence. With a universally designed learning environment, learners will be safe from the potholes of trauma.

Trauma-responsive learning environments restore power to the learner. As Najavits (2019) writes, "No one chooses trauma: whether it's a car accident, assault, natural disaster, sexual violence, or other trauma, the person was powerless to escape. Empowerment is thus hugely important. It means 'to give power.' It's about having options, choosing what's best for you, saying yes to what helps and no to what doesn't" (p. 57).

Barriers in Urban Schools

This is not a book explicitly about urban schools—racism happens everywhere and the disadvantages facing Black and Brown students follow them everywhere. But the reality is that many Black and Brown students attend struggling urban schools. In the largest 100 cities in the United States, students of color are much more likely to attend schools where most of their peers are Black or Brown and poor (Boschma & Brownstein, 2016). According to the National Center for Education Statistics (NAEP, 2015), "On average, white students attended schools that were 9 percent Black while Black students attended schools that were 48 percent Black, indicating a large difference in average Black student density nationally." Results also showed that schools in the highest density category (60 percent to 100 percent Black students) tended to be in cities.

The lists that urban schools find themselves included on are undesirable. Persistently low performing, lowest ranking, highest poverty index, state takeover/ receivership, highest suspensions and expulsions—these are some of the familiar lists where urban schools find the fellowship of scrutiny. Landing on these lists often leaves stakeholders scratching their heads wondering if anyone truly understands the plight of urban schools. With standardized tests being the one and only measure that matters to the ranking and evaluating of schools, urban educators are the ones defending, recovering, and trying to reinvigorate from the inside out. The battle-weary troops inside of urban schools wish desperately for the outside world to come and see what a day is like.

In just one day teachers encounter children who are hungry, children who are homeless, children in foster care, children who are struggling with the impact of trauma. For some children trauma paves the route to school with the number of abandoned homes, the high percentages of sex offenders on the streets, the threat of fighting and gang violence, the danger of entering an empty home. This reality weighs on the children when they walk through the door of the school. Imagine the stress, the worry, the anxiety, the debilitating pressure that comes with wondering if there is food to eat or clothes to wear or if the lights will be out again at home. These are just some of the realities facing students in urban areas.

Every day students in the urban schools must face the brutal facts: the standardized test expects you to normalize and perform—just like everyone else. With shrinking budgets and changing school finance formulas, schools are taking a beating. All schools are expected to do more with less. I once attended a conference where the speaker, leadership expert Rob Evans, said something that will always stick with me, "Schools have two jobs; to heal the sick and raise the dead." This is the plight of the urban school. Make the impossible possible for the unlikely regardless of what they are living in or living through. It feels impossible to mitigate the barriers of the urban environments, but there is hope that comes with practitioners who have high expectations of every student who walks through their doors. There is hope that rivals that of an emergency medical technician breathing life into a lifeless body as they perform CPR.

Urban teachers breathe into the life of every student. They administer the compressions with different methods, different incentives, and a different level of care. What urban teachers do is the difference between the emergency room and the morgue. It is the difference between the pipeline to college and careers or the pipeline to prison. Urban teachers are fully aware of the statistics, fully aware of the consequences, fully aware of the sanctions. But they consume themselves with the faces, the names, the stories, and the families who they serve with a tenacity that makes onlookers scoff and laugh.

About a year ago, a student that I had the privilege of teaching in both ninth and 11th grade reconnected with me. Chanay had become a cosmetologist, and now my daughter is her customer. Of course, during my daughter's appointments, we took time to catch up on what she was doing, how her road had changed from early childhood as a career path back to cosmetology. We laughed about funny stories from class and shared with each other where people were that we kept up with over the years.

Chanay said she had been in the honors program for years and struggled with feeling like she didn't belong. Describing the gifted and talented program, she felt like her intellect was invited, but her creativity was not. Can you imagine creativity being the force that fuels you to get up in the morning but having to put that unboxable beauty of your personality in a box until school is over? She described situation after situation that made her feel foreign, out of place, left out, and, quite frankly, not smart. I would have never guessed that she had those experiences before coming to high school.

Chanay was always vibrant, eager to participate, willing to reframe an assignment with the open options. I remember her going the extra mile with costumes, recordings, dance steps, and bringing characters to life. She was free in a way that allowed her to explore the content while unleashing the best characteristics about herself, not squelching them. Yes, with all of the pressures and issues going on around her she found a way to express her intellect and tap into her creativity, simply because the learning environment invited her to be her best self.

Mother Teresa once said about her work with the poor of Calcutta, India: "The biggest disease today is not leprosy or tuberculosis but rather the feeling of not belonging." I want every Chanay to be welcomed and challenged in our classrooms. Universal Design for Learning is the difference maker in changing the narrative of urban schools. Urban teachers see the conditions, the circumstances, and the crisis—and they roll up their sleeves and go to work. It is with this fearlessness that I want to introduce more urban teachers to the strategies of the successful urban teachers.

As an urban educator, you know the barriers that you and your students face, but you are also called to work with students and their families to eliminate them. Learners in urban areas are dealing with serious issues that certainly impact their educational experiences, including the high rates of crime and violence that accompany most cities and inner-ring suburbs. Writing in *Pediatrics*, Wade, Shea, Rubin, and Wood (2014) note that "Measuring adverse experiences is important for urban economically distressed children, who, in addition to experiencing poverty as an adversity, may be subjected to the experiences of abuse, neglect, and family dysfunction, along with a host of other stressors, including community violence, discrimination, and peer victimization."

I remember having my lesson plan interrupted because a student had lost her brother in a car accident, and again another had lost a brother to gun violence, and another student had gone too soon after a drug overdose. We started to count the connections, the sibling groups, the family ties, the tears that we knew we needed to wipe. We had to close the book and allow the learning community to grieve if we ever wanted the community to learn. It reminded me of what Jonathan Kozol (1991) wrote in *Savage Inequalities*:

> What is now encompassed by the one word ("school") are two very different kinds of institutions that, in function, finance and intention, serve entirely different roles. Both are needed for our nation's governance. But children in one set of schools are educated to be governors; children in the other set of schools are trained for being governed. The former are given the imaginative range to mobilize ideas for economic growth; the latter are provided with the discipline to do the narrow tasks the first group will prescribe (p. 212).

This dichotomy that Kozol describes speaks to the need for reform in America's urban schools. With concerns growing about the resegregation of schools and persistently low performing urban districts the need is pressing and daunting.

A quarter century ago, research by Lipman, Berman, and Macarthur (1996) showed that urban students had less family structure, economic security, housing stability, and access to medical care, and were more likely to engage in risky behavior, such as unprotected sex, that would make educational achievement harder to achieve. As Eric Jensen (2009) puts it: "The urban poor deal with a complex aggregate of chronic and acute stressors (including crowding, violence and noise) and are dependent on often-inadequate large-city services."

Despite the complexities and inequalities of urban living and or poverty, the outcome expectations are largely the same as their suburban and well-off counterparts. Students in urban areas are subject to the same assessment system that each state government has selected. In many cases ACT and SAT scores are reviewed for college acceptance consideration. Families in urban areas are depending on the services of urban schools to partner with them to build success stories regardless of the complexities of urban living.

Urban teachers and leaders are charged with the difficult task to find a road that is not barricaded by facts and statistics and lists and rankings. The revolutionaries of urban education guard the hopes and dreams of the students they serve. Rather than viewing the statistics as a life sentence, they are a springboard releasing learners to dream of success and actualize it.

With the UDL framework school communities will not be bound to the symptomology of a ZIP code or socioeconomic status. Students will realize the American dream as this framework releases educational excellence that echoes the words of our pledge to the flag "with liberty and justice for all." UDL releases stories of truth about our students. It gives them ways to learn, ways to lead, and ways to shine. It cures the loneliness of being singled out for failure. Learners get to shine, communities get to change their vantage point on schools, and parents get to believe in the possibility of better for their child no matter where they are located. This is the power of UDL: not a silver bullet but a set of promising practices that invite all students to choose, to speak, and to be truly heard. They get to belong by choice, not be placed on a list that everyone is running away from. They get to choose an amazing tomorrow because urban teachers open the door for them to shine today.

Reflection

1. Make a list of the initiatives or changes you have encountered in your educational experience. How many have had a lasting impact? Share your thoughts on why the initiatives made an impact or failed.

2. What issues outside of school are students and families struggling with that impact their academic performance? How can you start planning for those students specifically to minimize the barriers they are facing?

3. What stood out to you about Universal Design for Learning? What are you looking forward to learning more about?

4. Think about a learner that you are struggling to reach. What is their name? How much do you know about their story? What barriers are present for the learner? Keep them in mind as you read this book and think of them as you decide which strategies to try.

Engagement as License to Learn

In many instructional models it is up to the teacher to always be engaging, to always find the methods, to dig for all the materials, to teach everything. The UDL framework empowers students to drive themselves, to monitor themselves, to use feedback to improve themselves and then to make choices to ensure they are moving in the desired direction at all times. We dishonor them when we limit their choices and make them depend on us for all decision making. We also free ourselves by realizing that our primary job is to activate the motivation and purpose at the core of every learner.

Honoring our students by implementing UDL empowers Black and Brown students to shine as they experience academic, behavioral, and social-emotional success. With practice, they become expert learners who are motivated and purposeful to reach their goals. By providing multiple means of engagement, we teach students how to struggle and "fail forward" while practicing self-regulation. Additionally, we have the power and privilege to model learning and the power of engagement by fostering collaboration and community and learning right alongside them. In a UDL classroom, where engagement is paramount, students learn how they learn best and take charge of their learning.

Students in charge of their learning shift the teacher's role from owner of the knowledge to facilitator of resources for their students. It is such a place of power for our students. I feel like it is appropriate to quote the great scholar Spiderman to remind every one of us, "With great power comes great responsibility." Spiderman is teaching us to value the power that being in charge of learning brings. UDL is giving us the tools to be responsible and accountable with that power to make sure that teaching and learning is an accelerant toward life goals, not a deterrent or an insurmountable obstacle in the middle of the road.

We honor our students by empowering their brilliance. That word brilliance seems loaded at first. It is true that every student is brilliant in some way. Classrooms have to be places where our students' brilliance is not just welcomed but invited and celebrated.

Utilizing UDL practices gets the students prepared to drive on the expressway, not just practice. Getting out onto the actual expressway accelerates students toward their life goals not just the academic endeavors we have in mind for them.

Engagement is so much more than recruiting student interest. It's about creating an environment that is rigorous and support-ive so all students have equal opportunities to challenge them-selves, reach high expectations, and see themselves as scholars, capable of greatness. To do this, it is critical that we minimize threats and distractions, commit to being trauma-informed, and create conditions that nurture the brilliance of our students. If we do not recognize how threatening and racist our systems are, we are serving environments that prevent our Black and Brown students from learning. Consider the following analogy.

Imagine walking down a dark alley. You feel like it may be dangerous, but you also feel like you have no alternatives to get where you are going. There isn't much light, just a flickering bulb in a streetlight that is casting shadows right as you walk. There are sounds that you really don't recognize, but you have to keep walking. There is no other choice. As you walk you hear the sounds of voices. You turn around but don't see anyone there. You pull your hood down so that you can see more clearly— just in case. You arrest the thought of the danger—the possibilities— and just keep walking. You hear some shuffling and turn around in just enough time to see a cat scurrying through some leaves. You pick up your pace, just a bit and begin thinking that your car is nearby. "Just get to the car. Just get to the car," You chant to yourself as motivation.

As you near the end of this tight passageway you see that your car is in sight. You hear what is undoubtedly footsteps behind you. You pick up the pace to a jog. You hear hurried breathing and turn around to see someone barreling toward you as quickly as they possibly can. You are not sure if you will make it to your car. You are not sure if this is a life of death situation. Your muscles are tense. Your adrenaline soars. Your mind races as you wonder …

Pause: Do you feel that? That feeling of uncertainty and terror? Do you feel that heart that is creating an earthquake in your chest? Do you feel the loss of certainty that feeling of becoming a slave to the unknown? It's a horrible scene—not knowing what will happen, feeling trapped in the circumstance, powerless against what may happen next, subject to the person that you just can't escape. Typing this I can feel my anxiety going through the roof. I don't wish this scenario on my worst enemy. Can you imagine this feeling?

Let's switch the scene from a dark alley to a room bright with fluorescent lights, decorated with bulletin boards and filled with peers all the same age as you. Suddenly without warning your name is called from the front of the room. The ten seconds of silence feel like a torture chamber, and just when you thought it couldn't get worse Jimmy makes that snickering noise that triggers all out laughter from Lorelai. Torture turns to terror and your name is called again. Yelled this time. "Pay attention! This is important!!"

Your mind races as you try to calculate the number of minutes until this day is over. Forty-five minutes. You try to listen. You try to put your head down to collect your thoughts. You hear footsteps and you know that the teacher is coming near your desk. This is your last chance to get out before—who knows what will happen. Trapped. Stuck. Nowhere to go. No one to help. Alone. And the lesson goes on.

How much of the lesson do you think you would retain right after the alley scenario, or the classroom one? How willing would you be to answer a question or to participate in a group activity? I wouldn't be able to accomplish very much, but it's not a lack of resilience. Something happens in the brain when there is fear. The work of University of Chicago researcher Micere Keels (2018) shows that it interferes with critical thinking and problem solving. We must not allow our classrooms to be places of fear. There cannot be engagement if there is fear. There cannot be engagement when there is racism. Students cannot take academic risks in a classroom that is not antiracist and safe.

The idea of risk is one that can make or break a student. In the book *The Coaching Habit: Say Less, Ask More & Change the Way You Lead Forever,* Stanier (2016), introduced me to the research about the TERA Quotient. The TERA Quotient explains the neuroscience behind what happens when people feel like they are at risk or in danger. The implications for the classroom are far reaching. Part of honoring students is decreasing their risks by providing options that communicate that the classroom is a safe place for all students.

Universal Design for Learning practices reduce the fight or flight mindset that comes with students feeling like they are in danger and increases their access to learning is extremely exciting. The TERA Quotient takes into account the following four factors:

- T is for Tribe, and the question the brain is asking is this: Are you with me, or against me?

- E is for Expectation, and the question here is: Do I know what's about to happen, or don't I?

- R is for Rank, where the question is: Whose status is higher, yours or mine?

- A is for Autonomy, where the brain is checking out: How much say do I have here?

Classrooms evoke an emotional response right away that impacts each student's ability to truly engage. It doesn't matter how amazingly decorated or how super organized the room is. In a blog, "Three Habits to Have Your People with You, Not Against You" (Box of Crayons, 2016), the authors note that sensing danger places people in a fighting stance. The brain starts working on protection from the situation. If the brain senses that the environment is safe than an ability to truly engage emerges. Because we want our classrooms to be safe zones where the brain is free to thrive we have to be intentional and masterful at minimizing threats (Table 5.1). UDL practices decrease the threat response that keeps the brain from functioning in a way that learning is possible and plausible.

Table 5.1: Practices to Communicate Safety and Increase the TERA Quotient (Stanier, 2016)

T—Tribe. What communicates to students that they are a part of my tribe?	• Give intentional greetings.
	  o Call each student by name upon entry.
	  o Offer specialized handshakes.
	• Emphasize communal responsibility.
	• Ask students how they are doing and listen for an answer.
	• Ask follow-up questions from the day before.

Continued on the next page

Table 5.1: (*Continued*)

	• Celebrate birthdays simply. • Sit with students, get down to their level, stand beside not over them. • Welcome back any student who was absent. • Check in on students in a way that is non-threatening.
E is for Expectation. Do students know what's about to happen?	• Put the agenda on the board, or in an online shared drive. • Post expectations. • Review expectations often. • Teach students how to transition from one activity to another. • Clearly communicate options for assignments. • Show videos, offer visuals, or written directions of how to successfully move through the assignment or tasks. • Identify the expectation for each person's contribution. • Be specific about how the assignment will be evaluated. • Review often what will happen before, during and after an assignment. • Explain often which areas of the assignment are flexible and which are non-negotiable. • Invite questions about tasks and process. • Model what to do if students come to a road block. • Use a timer that is both audible and visual to alert students to how much time is remaining.

Table 5.1: *(Continued)*

Rank. How can you communicate that students have a high status in your classroom?	• Adjust proximity to move closer. • Have a seat. Don't always stand and deliver. • Invite students to take leadership and ownership. • Be willing to learn from students. • Ask for feedback. • Enlist student leadership with class meetings.
Autonomy brings a feeling of safety. How do you communicate to students that they have a voice that matters in your classroom?	• Invite participation in multiple formats (speaking, texting, emailing, electronic polls, etc.). • Ask for suggestions often. • Provide flexibility with assignment options. • Give choices for how to show what they know. • Allow time to research topics of interest. • Offer multiple pathways to the same outcome. • Offer alternatives to activities. • Let students give input when creating assignments. • Allow students to choose how and when they consult resources for help. • Compile a resource bank of supports ahead of time so that students will have what they need to move forward with or without assistance. • Record audio help or video help to assist the students. They can select when and how they use the help if they need it.

Fostering engagement in all learners, especially those for whom the system was not built, like our brilliant Black and Brown students, is both an art and a science. Community members, parents and students esteem the role of teacher without embracing the responsibility of being a learner. The beauty of the art and science of teaching is that educators are lifelong learners. Students come into the classroom expecting to be told what to learn and how to learn. A teacher who honors the students sets an environment where teachers expect to be a part of the learning community. The teacher expects to give valuable knowledge but also expects to receive valuable knowledge from the students. Learners in this classroom will know four things:

1. You didn't come here empty handed. Every student brings something to the table. They have experiences and/or background knowledge that will enhance and enrich every learner in the classroom community.

2. You are welcomed and valuable. Every student makes this classroom community special. Your ideas, your questions, your personality, your talents, and your curiosity make this community unique and valuable to the entire world. We want you here! We need you here.

3. You will teach, share, and grow to learn. Learning is not just listening to the teacher and taking a test. Learning is teaching. Learning is sharing how you learn just as much as what you learn. Learning is tracking your growth and owning your story. You have a responsibility for your learning.

4. Your destination is important. Your goals are a priority in our learning community. Your destination matters. Share your life goals or your life question so that we can all work together to put this learning experience to work for you! We are collectively responsible for making sure we take steps ahead to our goals.

In a UDL community we are diligent to receive what each learner has to give. We teach all learners to receive from each other respectfully by modeling receptiveness graciously in the classroom.

Sharing the learning responsibility with your students can be daunting, but if you are to truly build student engagement, you must. There is a chance that students, in their attempt to present their understanding, may share incorrect information. Because we are all human beings, there is a chance for error when we learn as well. How do we mitigate that risk? Preparation. Here are some practical things you can do to ensure that as students self-differentiate, they also reflect and review.

1. Utilize an information protocol for learners to view and listen. With the information protocol, other community members will become built in fact checkers. This encourages research, information literacy and other critical thinking skills in the context of collaboration and community.

2. Encourage a "Three Before Me" policy for review. Have three members of the learning community walk through your work and give feedback on how to improve. Utilize a rubric or review guidelines to calibrate responses. Make sure that the person who gives feedback has guidelines for responding and earns credit for their peer review.

3. Submit work to an authentic audience whenever possible. Write editorials and letters to community or world changers, comment on scholarly blogs, enter science fairs; record video blogs, YouTube videos, and songs to share. Receive their genius and encourage the rest of the world to do the same. When students are preparing for the scrutiny of the real world as an audience, their level of effort to attain accuracy will be heightened.

No matter how many choices and options you have for students there may be a few who just aren't feeling it. This is not the time to drop an anvil from teacher heaven and make them get in line or get out. This is truly the beauty of the UDL learning environment. It is normal to have students who are more comfortable in a traditional setting, where there are no options and many specific and strict directions. A UDL learning environment still has a great deal of structure, but there are options and choices within the structure. In order to scaffold students into UDL, perhaps you can provide a limited number of choices to give them an opportunity to try new things. Also, If a student doesn't want to participate in activities that are more UDL style, then make provisions for them to give input on the existing options, or suggest an option of their own with your help or the help of a classmate. UDL is fully collaborative and fully customizable to meet the diverse learning styles and needs of all students, not just some. Even reluctant students will find a way to shine with a little support and guidance with their newfound freedom to guide their own learning.

Engagement in Our Black and Brown Communities

Each community has distinguishing factors, assets, history, and character. As a teacher and/or leader in a community that serves Black and Brown children, we have a responsibility to encourage students to recognize any assets in the community that will accelerate them on the road to their dream.

Each community tells a story. A story of the past, of generational significance, of future possibilities, of intersections, and forks in the road. Unfortunately, studying can also show the ugly roots of racism through redlining, gentrification, and community divesting. No matter what the story of the community, it is important to connect to perspectives that may be lesser known and even hidden. Whether the history that is uncovered is rich and filled with pride or has troubling or ugly implications—we must know it and own it to serve our learners well.

W. Kamau Bell, a comedian and political journalist, uses his show "United Shades of America" to find challenges in American communities and explore them from different viewpoints and perspectives. When I watch his show, I am amazed by how limited my view is when I don't consider someone else's viewpoint or argument. It enriches me to know someone else's story, especially people who are within my circle of influence. Think about the power of exploring the history, resources, and assets of the neighborhood where you work and serve. Imagine the power of learning the history, the challenges and the victories from various perspectives. The funds of knowledge that we can connect to, the cultural storehouses that lend to building bridges and the contextual enrichening that is needed to reach Black and Brown students is often unlocked when we place ourselves as learners to an experience we would otherwise not be able to access. The choice to listen and learn yields great rewards for educators and learners alike.

My husband used to tell me I needed one of those bumper stickers that says, "Warning: This vehicle makes frequent stops." He was right. When I saw my students or their families it was very common for me to pull over and have a conversation or jump out and walk with them a bit. I was known for rolling up on my students if I saw them smoking a cigarette in the bus stop, even if they were far away from the school or if it was the weekend.

I know the back streets, the side streets, the cut throughs, the walkways. I know our community. I've learned our community and I recognize that I still have a great deal to learn. Are you willing to learn about the community where you serve as an educator? Are you willing to learn about the community from a Black and Brown perspective, or various socioeconomic perspectives? It may be uncomfortable, but we can't serve well those who we fear or pity. We serve best when we are willing to walk a mile in our learners' shoes or at least take a walk that traces their steps.

Do you know your neighborhood?

This activity can be completed with a team of teachers or individually. Every invitation to learn starts with a benefit. The answer to "Why are we doing this?" has to be deeply embedded into the work that the work itself motivates you to keep working, keep searching, stay focused, find answers and even garner a whole new set of questions for later. The invitation to this kind of learning opens up many opportunities to connect and build for future learning experiences.

Early in my preservice teaching courses, my cohort was given an assignment. So we broke into teams, with disposable cameras and tried our best to learn the community where we would be teaching. We took note of landmarks, businesses, restaurants, monuments, alleys, laundromats, corner stores, lampposts, home conditions, apartment buildings and community centers. We asked ourselves questions like, "What is this community known for? How has it changed? What will our students pass to get here every day?" So, we probably looked like silly tourists, but we learned so many things that day.

Here's a challenge: Think about the city where you teach as a tourist location. What are the landmarks? Where are the historical markers? What are the brag points? What are the areas for growth?

Don't just think about the answers. Choose one of these methods to gain the information you need:

- Use a web-based map service to find pictures of as many of the landmarks listed as possible.

- Drive around the city. Get out and go into the places you find.

- Walk the streets that your students take every day to and from school taking note of the landmarks and important places.

Try It!

Community Treasure Hunt

Every destination begins right where you are! Do you know where you are?

The underpinning of excellence in education is foundationally set upon our beliefs and values. This activity will equip you with community gems both known and unknown that will help you know and serve your students. Getting to know our community, building a network of assistance, and making personal connections will lead us to the ultimate goal of achieving our district vision and mission.

Whether you are new to the district or have been here for many years, discovering our city will help you discover hidden gems and celebrate the great services offered here. You will participate in a Community Treasure Hunt. Document your journey with pictures, short video clips and signatures in your passport document. There are a number of stops you will make but take note of what you see as you drive, walk or digitally visit from one point to another.

- Landmarks, monuments

- Stores, Supermarkets, Local Businesses, Factories

- Restaurants

- Places of worship

- Possible places for community service

- City Hall

- Playgrounds

- Meeting Spaces
- Community Resource Agencies
- Community Centers
- Police stations, fire department and public safety buildings
- Places that make the community unique
- Barber shops/ Beauty salons
- Libraries
- Dream mines—places that are not in service but with partners and vision would enhance the community

Option A. Create a song and a music video/slide show tour of our city.

Option B. Create a map of the city with a legend to the places that have been identified. Extra credit—Create an additional dream pitch for one of the dream mines you find while walking the city.

Option C. Create a bank of resources for the family/ parent liaison in the district to share with families with brochures.

Option D. Break into competing teams and use the fifteen items as a scavenger hunt. The first team to secure pictures at each kind of location wins. Extra points will be awarded if you get a person from the establishment to pose with a sign that says, "I Believe in insert name of school or district."

Option E. Write an editorial to the local newspaper about all the great places in your city. Extra credit for submitting the article for publication

If you have an idea for another option, please share it!

Questions for reflection:

- How could this information help you to teach more effectively?

- What connections with your grade level standards and/or subject matter did you find in the neighborhood?

- When listening to what other teams saw, did you miss anything in the neighborhood?

- What does this tell you about collaboration?

After you get to know your community, you have to know your families. Parents have a vested interest in their child's success whether they are in urban schools or elsewhere. One administrator reminded her staff that, "Parents send the best child they can to school each day." Communication is the key to parent buy-in. Share with them the goals, methods, and endless opportunities. Give parents a few examples of options, let them view a few samples of lesson variations, let them see a few final projects. The most important part to parent buy-in is inviting them to dream with you.

Host a parent or caregiver think tank, where you learn their dreams for their children. You also brainstorm their willingness to partner with you or connect you with those who may want to help you throughout the year. Student led conferences are also very helpful. Parents often have very demanding schedules so find as many ways to connect with parents as possible. There are many legitimate reasons that parents are unavailable for traditional conferences. Parents may not be able to call off work or find child care for their younger children. Some parents may have found conferences to be a waste of time in the past or feel intimidated by school experiences. Plan ahead for each unique parent situation. Try some of these alternatives to traditional face to face conferences because our families need options and choices just as much as our students:

1. Video check-in. A student creates a video recording of their progress on a certain topic or skill. The teacher chimes in briefly at the end giving ideas for next steps or additional opportunities for practice and or publication.

2. Break time breakdown. Offer a live stream of a presentation or video so that parents can log in from wherever they are and view.

3. Add the parent as a collaborator on Google Docs so that they can see their child's progress in real time.

4. For parental input, request parents to upload an encouraging video to their child that you can play for them as a surprise or whenever motivation is needed.

5. Record audio updates with the student and send them to the parent.

6. Get electronic feedback on projects utilizing an online survey.

7. Offer traditional conferencing or training on various ways to stay connected to the classroom.

These are a few ideas to help parents have a better understanding of the structure of your classroom and the benefits of the UDL framework. Get ideas from them on communication and encourage new ideas that will increase their awareness of what is happening in the classroom particularly as it relates to their child's progress. Valuing parents sets the stage for a true partnership that breaks down barriers between school and home. We need family involvement to serve our Black and Brown students well. Building bridges between home and school empowers Black and Brown families to empower learners toward success with the school as an ally.

The Power of Getting Out of the Way

The greatest honor a teacher can bestow upon a student is to receive learning from them. To get out of the driver's seat and invite the student to not only drive, but to drive the teacher speaks to two elements of community in the classroom.

I trust you enough to teach me. I trust you enough to teach others

When you became licensed to drive, the person who taught you had the most confidence in what you could do. Because they taught you, they were keenly aware of your areas of strength and your areas of weakness. My driving instructor was Mrs. Foote. After several sessions with her she was very confident in my street driving skills. In fact, she was a great deal more confident in me than I was. She would give me ridiculous directions and commands just to give me more experience on the road. She had no problem getting in the passenger seat because she knew that I would listen to her and drive carefully and cautiously. When I received my license, I thought my mother would be excited to let me drive her car. Because she had never driven with me, she didn't know my skill level or trust my skill level. She was afraid to let me drive alone or with anyone else.

Similarly, in the classroom the more we know a student's skills and push them toward new levels of learning and demonstration of learning—the more comfortable we will be relinquishing the control of the driver's seat for them to gain the confidence and expertise that the real world requires. My mom didn't trust my driving then, but she also hadn't had the chance to see me in action.

We are accountable to one another

Universal Design for Learning is a framework that fosters creativity and innovative thinking but not at the expense of student achievement. It is a way to enhance rigor, increase effectiveness, and intensify teaching and learning for a lifetime. While this approach does invite the natural brilliance of each student to shine, it also causes each member of the learning community to stretch and build on their natural gifts. The brilliance that your students walk in the classroom with should not be the only brilliance they leave the classroom with.

The goal of a UDL environment is to use their natural brilliance as a foundation of sorts. A giant hole that fortifies the building structure. As they learn to fill their foundation with knowledge, then they build on their brilliance by learning how to communicate their new learning. They connect new pieces to the foundation by expanding their understanding, making connections, sharing what they know, and seeking out what they don't. It is imperative to keep the goal of student achievement at the forefront. Keep asking: Are you learning? Are you growing? How do you know? How can we work together to get you farther faster? Document the story every step of the way.

Expert learners drive their own learning. Engaged learners can drive because they have a purpose that is connected to a goal that is valuable to them. They understand how this learning serves them well and they make choices to stay motivated with the purpose in mind. Teachers get a chance to coach learners in this area and structure learning experiences that help them build this muscle.

Teacher Engagement Is Important, Too

Take a step back from the work and ask yourself, "Am I growing? Am I learning?" Fostering student achievement is greatly enhanced by keeping a fresh perspective on what it means to be a learner. Albert Einstein said, "Once you stop learning you start dying." Corpses are known for a great number of things, but teaching is not one of them. Keeping a fresh perspective on how you learn and what methods of instruction are most effective for your own learning catapults you into a mode of reflection that enhances your personal practice.

Learning from someone else also gives you an opportunity to receive from someone else. There is honor in that. A teacher who is not only willing, but able to become a student has a credibility with learners that is steeped in the humility of allowing the shine to be shared in the room. To hop on the Einstein bandwagon, I would like to add—the decision to keep learning is the decision to keep living. A decision to keep living through learning is the clearest pathway to elevating your effectiveness in teaching.

Teachers who are engaged learners are powerful. They elevate their practice and their prowess by surrendering to a tender truth that all the answers are not within one person. They lay down the power in the front of the room and set ablaze the minds and hearts of others in their presence simply by offering them the invitation to use their voices, minds, and creativity to teach another.

Who is licensed to learn? Who is commissioned to be a student? Who is authorized to be a teacher? Every person in the learning community who seeks to learn also bears the great responsibility of releasing knowledge through teacher, sharing, collaborating, and contributing.

Excellence in teaching Black and Brown learners through an antiracist and universally designed lens starts by valuing the community of the students you serve and working to design environments that both honor those communities, reflect their values, and create conditions of nurture and engagement. Also, by valuing yourself as a vehicle for excellence and change where many have deemed it impossible. You get the honor of breaking the ground of transformation by the questions you ask, the assignments you give, the expectations you promote, the support that you make available. You get to honor the history of the community by connecting the dots to the future—the future that you serve through powerful connected instruction using multiple means of engagement.

Reflection

- Am I growing as a teacher? Am I learning? How do I know?

- Have I asked my students what instructional strategies have best served them in their learning? What were the results? How does this help me? What will I change? What will I sustain?

- What students have taught me something new? What was my response?

- Who have I shared my students' expertise with?

- How can I capture what I have learned about teaching these concepts to preserve for other teachers and other learners? Before you build a map to where you are going, take stock of where you are. Imagine better schools, better communities, and a better world not by asking "Where are you going?" but by pausing, acknowledging, and celebrating where you are right now.

- What would happen if students and teachers felt like each person in the learning community was worthy of sharing their brilliance?

- What would happen if students and teachers were willing to receive each other's feedback with the weight of value that respect and honor carries?

CHAPTER 6

Representation
Honoring by Invitation

"I don't get it," Hannah mutters to herself as she slams her notebook closed. She looks at the words and symbols on the board and figures this must be what it is like to be in a country and not be able to speak the language. She had missed a few days last week because she had had an asthma attack. Anytime the coughing turns to wheezing and her inhaler doesn't calm the symptoms, she knows she might end up in the emergency room. Her apartment has three problems that make her asthma worse: carpet, a smoker next door, and moisture that is turning to mold. After a few days in the hospital filled with medications and breathing treatments, she was released.

Now, sitting in Math class, Hannah can't seem to find her way back to the path of understanding. Missing school a few days every month or every other month due to illness has taken its toll on her understanding. In other classes she can find her way back quickly, but in Math class she feels lost. Over two years she has missed close to 60 days of school.

She shifts in her seat and takes a deep breath "I really have no idea what's going on here," she whispers to her friend Cherish.

Whether it is from being absent, a little late to class, or just not making the connection to the content there is nothing worse than that feeling of being lost. Many times our Black and Brown students experience this feeling, not because they don't know the material, but because curriculum writers and text book authors write for a white audience and very rarely are purposeful or inclusive of Black or Brown voices. This creates a critical barrier. The U.S. Department of Education (2020) does report that Black and Brown children account for 37.5% of chronically absent students, while white students account for about 14.5%. Whether it is absenteeism, learning differences, or cultural exclusion, we have to use multiple means of representation to invite our students to the content in various ways.

Cherish opens her laptop and clicks into the corresponding lesson for the day. "Do you have your headphones?" Hannah nods her head and laughs because Cherish always has a quick solution when she is struggling. As soon as the lesson opening is over, she shows her the connection quiz that they had done a little earlier. The quiz was available in print or online. There were questions about pizza, wheels on car, clocks on a wall, and a Ferris wheel. She was slightly familiar with the term Ferris wheel but clicked on the hyperlink just to make sure that she was thinking of the same thing as the quiz. There was a picture of the ride that she hates at the carnival that sets up in her neighborhood every summer.

"I got stuck at the top of a Ferris wheel one time," she confides in Cherish. "I hate those things."

"Well, if it is a circle, we are going to be talking about them in Math so get ready."

"Oooh, did you talk about hula hoops already? That's a circle!" Her eyes light up and Cherish says, "Now you have turned into the teacher on me!" They giggle as they sort through the resources. Some are electronic, some hang up around the room, some are on the board, and others are used by students in the room. The picture on the board of a circle with a dot in the middle labeled A and a line connecting it to a point on the outer circle labeled B is starting to make a little sense. But the equations $(x - h)^2 + (y - k)^2 = r^2$ and $x^2 + y^2 + Dx + Ey + F = 0$ are still foggy for her.

Hannah watches a video about defining circles and gains perspective on the definition and the center point. She finds herself humming along to the music video that shares the definitions of radius, diameter, and circumference. The pictures on the teacher's presentations are also hyperlinked to standalone definitions, examples, and other resources. Her classmates post helpful resources and share pictures on the interactive bulletin board on what helps them to understand the terms and vocabulary. Hannah chooses a few to get her started and then listens to a few more circle songs from the playlist that her teacher prepared. There are all styles of music, but she chooses what is interesting to her. She looks at the problems for the day and uses videos, playdough, graphing paper, a needle and thread, and a ruler to test out her knowledge. Knowing three points on a circle, can she figure out the center point? That is the question of the day.

Honoring our students by creating opportunities to customize our instruction celebrates learning needs and learning differences instead of shunning them. Providing multiple means of representation shows students that you have thought ahead about their background knowledge and experience, community and cultural references, and other aids to understanding which communicates a strong desire to see the entire community of learners succeed. This is honor.

Meyer, Rose, and Gordon (2014) note that a "simple affirmation of learners' positive sense of self, of their value as individuals, and the importance of their membership in a cultural tradition has repeatedly been shown to have positive effects on learning and on performance" (p. 57). If we want to reach the rigorous and lofty goals of improving academic achievement, then we have to be mindful and action oriented to provide options that meet the needs of varying learners in our classrooms.

If you have ever been on the expressway, you know that on-ramps are the main route to access them. On-ramps are paths that are literally created in an area, where there once was nothing, to get you on the road to your destination, from your current location in a convenient and quick manner. Even though very few people have on-ramps that lead directly to their driveways, the whole purpose is to find an on-ramp that is nearest to you and that serves your purpose intentionally. Guiding students toward becoming expert learners is like choosing to build an on-ramp to the expressway of learning. Where there are barriers to learning, we get to build on-ramps that eliminate or overtake the barriers by providing options that awaken the background knowledge, connect to current information, and propels them forward to explore with an informed sense of confidence and curiosity.

My family recently returned from a very long road trip. We spent about 30 hours on the road over a span of 5 days. At one point, the windshield was so covered with dirty water that had dried while we were driving that it was difficult to see. The covering of the windshield happened gradually so it was hard to even see that our vision was being obstructed. We thought something was wrong with our eyes until we realized that the dirty windshield was the problem.

Students who are in classrooms where there are limited options for perception, language, mathematical expressions, symbols, or comprehension are sitting behind muddy windshields. Instead of recognizing the barriers, they are making harsh judgments about their ability to learn. What if the only representation Hannah could use was what was written on the board? What if there were no options that appealed to her interests or tapped into her background knowledge?

Far too many Black and Brown children sit through lessons that are based on the teacher's interest or the examples in the text. We have to create avenues for them to customize the experience. Providing options is like clearing the mud and muck away from windshields. The customized display helps students see the content clearly. Learners realize that the support to clarify and decode helps them see the road ahead with much more clarity and activates an enthusiasm to continue. Providing multiple means of representation removes barriers by helping students see the learning that needs to happen. More importantly it helps students to see themselves as capable and competent learners.

Think about Hannah or other students whose challenges you are aware of. As we look at some examples of the guidelines in action, begin the process of constructing practical on-ramps for your universally designed learning environment. Before we build an on-ramp let's take a look at the barriers that limit access to learning.

Perception is the way that learners take in information. Whether the information is best perceived through hearing, seeing, touching, experiencing or some combination, classrooms often present only one format. Even if the one presented format may be a method that works well for you as a learner, we cheat students from experiencing the content in a variety of ways when we limit the power of choice. Hannah had the opportunity to use technology to view videos, definitions, pictures and songs. She also had the opportunity to use words and pictures created by other learners as support. There manipulatives for her to see the learning in actions by creating a circle with playdough and finding the center, then plugging in the numbers and seeing if the formula gave her the same response. She had a chance to think about circles in her world before solving problems for circles in her class. She used the resources available to her and others so that she could find her way back to the content. Multiple means of representation gives learners a chance to find their way.

In the first course that I took on UDL there were often various options for perceiving or taking in content. Because I wanted to ensure that I understood the research correctly, I often consumed the content in all formats that were available. All students won't do that, but some students may learn bits and pieces from each format presented, or they may get everything they need from one. They are able to choose the format, or control options within the format like sound and text size for their personal perception. Multiple means of representation are there for learners to decide where and how to get on the road of learning regardless of ability, preference, challenge or situation.

Learners need space to figure out the most effective method of perceiving information for their learning. By simply making a choice, learners will practice strategizing and reflecting to ensure that they are moving the direction of the desired outcome. Black and Brown children need spaces to strategize their practice. They need room to engage with resources that they can connect with. Do your resources include culturally accessible questions and scenarios that will activate or supply background knowledge? Do Black and Brown children get a chance to connect and visualize the concepts in real life? Are their lives invited to the learning? Are there resources available to give insight to experiences that may not be commonplace? Are there multiple on ramps to the content like movies, music, poetry, pictures that give learners choices on where to start to get to the desired destination?

Think about One Standard and Give It 5!

Try remixing your instruction to provide the same content five different ways as an on-ramp to multiple means of representation.

- Create an infographic to pair text with non-linguistic clues about the content.

- Blog the content with hyperlinks to related readings and electronic activities.

- Make an audio recording of the content or connect text with an electronic reader.

- Sing a song about the content make the lyrics available for learners to sing along.

- Build in supports such as glossaries and/or formula sheets for ready references.

Consider making your message sticky by changing the words to a popular or classic song. Try your hand at creating a few alternatives for auditory options like podcasts, radio shows or character speeches. Teaching students how to navigate technology with text readers or noise canceling headphones may also be a power move for creating a UDL on-ramp in your learning environment. The fun part is that for many topics these resources may already exist, and teachers and learners alike get to become curators of content to support their own learning.

Think about Background Knowledge and Context

I remember assigning my students a reading comprehension selection taken from a standardized test. The sample was beautifully written about wildfires in Yellowstone Park. I read the passage and used the worldview that I had to deduce some interesting facts about what might be happening here. When I went over the passage with my students, one raised his hand and asked, "How did the stones turn yellow and how could stones burn down?" I gave him a look that communicated my puzzlement. He went on to explain that he had used information from the text to help him figure out what Yellowstone was.

From the title he thought Yellowstone was a national park of, you guessed it, large yellow stones. Looking through the passage he used everything he had at his disposal to work through this passage. He used the words, the title, the footnotes. He used the skills that I had taught him to read, and envision, and use the headers and the footers. But there was an assumption about Yellowstone that the test makers and those who selected the passage forgot to share. Yes, it was a national park, but it wasn't until the eighth paragraph that the author mentions that Yellowstone Park had forests. So my student wasn't dumb, he wasn't disabled, he wasn't clueless. What was being measured put him at a distinct disadvantage—he hadn't traveled to the West. He had never been to Wyoming. He didn't have a worldview that gave him an expansive knowledge of the world. Perhaps if there was a question about the Great Lakes he would have a context for it, but this was not the case.

It was eye opening to me that students without opportunities to travel and be exposed to various ecosystems in the world, or national landmarks were at a distinct disadvantage than those who have had these experiences. Many states are acknowledging that there are biases in the way tests are written and assembled. The beauty of our classrooms is that we get to create learning experiences that honor our students' experiences; that build on where they are; that exposes them virtually to things they would otherwise never experience. We get to create on-ramps to the expressway of learning.

Make It Visual

Make your classroom rich with visuals and be sure that those visuals represent the identities in your classroom. An antiracist educator remembers that the walls of your classroom, the pictures in the presentation slides, the voices in your audio books all send a message about worth and acceptance to your learners. Educators teach all students how to honor Black and Brown voices as worthy when we consistently incorporate pictures, art, quotes, that reflect the weight of that sentiment. If we only decorate with Black and Brown faces during Black

History Month, we do a disservice to the body of work that is available, complex, and academically appropriate to communicate from and interact with the standards.

A few visual methods to use will go a long way in honoring students. You may not think of yourself as an artist, but you must be a learner. For example, try creating a Prezi that engages learners with a visual path for learning. Key ideas are easily highlighted. You may also want to try your hand at graphic design on Canva.com. There are many free premade designs that can be customized for your content. Using visual methods as a means of representation electronically will empower learners to enlarge, enhance or change the color of the images in ways that are helpful for their own learning. Creating animated vignettes of the content with websites like Powtoon (www.powtoon.com) can make the information accessible to students as well.

Format matters. Think creatively about ways to appeal to all senses for learning. Simply offering a variety of formats opens an on-ramp for learners to experiment and learn about the content, but also about themselves as learners. Customizing the display of information attracts students to the learning so that they can choose what works best for them. Even if their choice does not work well for them, or they don't understand the content, encourage learners to try other options to see if it clarifies their misunderstandings.

Provide Options for Language and Symbols

There are times that learners will need support to take in new information. Universally designed lessons consider the varying needs of learners and give them the power of choice in their supports. If they are watching a video on a new concept and come to a word they do not know, it is important to have a variety of supports to help them clarify vocabulary and symbols.

That can look different based on the content. Consider glossary sheets, or weblinks to the words that have been identified as frequently unknown. Technology offers learners a method to see the word, hear the word and read or listen to the word used in context. Offering strategies ahead of time for what to do when you meet unfamiliar words may also be helpful. Color coding words or having words in families that can be regrouped based on new learning gives students options for interacting with new words.

My son loves to create stories with new words to help him remember the definition. The vocabulary word that he had lots of fun with was prevaricate. He launched into a tall tale about being casted in the Broadway version of *Matilda* as he spoke to his grandfather on the phone. As Papa beamed with excitement, my son said, "This would be great, but it is all prevaricated." When Papa asked what is prevaricated, he refused to help him, but encouraged him to use clues or look it up. We are hoping that he uses his prevarication for good and not for evil in the coming days.

Simply utilizing pictures can open up the content to learners for whom text is a barrier. Pictures may make math formulas come alive or scientific concepts take shape in a learner's mind. Options for perception break the monotony of one size fits all and truly drops on-ramps in unlikely places to get every student on the road to learning. Math songs help explain the meaning of notations and symbols. Clarifying sentence structure and word relationships with reality show characters (think diagramming sentences meets TMZ) may help some students perceive the role of various parts of speech/ punctuation and how it changes the meaning of a group of words together. Utilizing multiple forms of media creates many paths for the learner empowered by choice.

Prioritize Comprehension

Providing options for comprehension can be done in many ways. I wrote this poem to invite my students to Comprehension Cafe:

Your background knowledge is welcome here
Remember that trip that you went on last year
Or that group of trees you pass every day
Or the members of your family that had something to say

Remember the activities that you did earlier this year
The charts, graphs, pictures, silly videos all here
The questions that we've answered and homework that's been done
Bring them out let's have a look remember all the fun

Process through our learning and graphic organizers guide
The posters, patterns, pictures, projects make your thoughts a slip and slide
We've cut and pasted memories now lets connect them to something new
Activating background knowledge is an on-ramp to learning for me and you!

Honoring our students by creating opportunities to customize our instruction celebrates learning differences instead of shunning them. Providing multiple means of representation shows students that you have thought ahead about their preferences and their struggles which communicates a strong desire to see all of them succeed. This is honor. "A simple affirmation of learners' positive sense of self, of their value as individuals, and the importance of their membership in a cultural tradition has repeatedly been shown to have positive effects on learning and on performance," write Meyer, Rose, and Gordon (2014, p. 57).

If we want to reach the rigorous and lofty goals of improving academic achievement, then we have to be mindful and action oriented to provide options that meet the needs of varying learners in our classrooms.

Use What You Have to Gain What You Don't

In a classroom that utilizes the Universal Design for Learning Guidelines teachers provide options for language, mathematical expressions, and symbols. These multiple means of representation provide on-ramps that provide clarity and support where misconceptions and misunderstandings had been barriers to learning. Each time you provide tools that give students access to vocabulary that may have been a stumbling block— you create an on-ramp.

Each time you provide an acronym or a pneumonic device that serves as a guide for how to decode text, and mathematical formulas or scientific symbols—you have torn down a barrier and built an on-ramp. When you have provided translations, pictures, songs, webtools that give the students the utensils needed to independently and resourcefully navigate the academic task at hand, you have just resourced them to gain knowledge in a distinctly customized fashion. By preparing for variability in your classroom you give more students access to the expressway of learning that has been excluded far too many for far too long. on-ramps don't create traffic jams, they simply get more people on the desired route to their personalized outcome.

Thinking ahead for the students you serve and crafting lessons that connect with each student creates on-ramps for all students, instead of just a few that respond to a particular style or method.

Albert Einstein was a genius, but he learned differently. He had difficulty recognizing the letter patterns and sound-symbol connections required for reading (Meyer, Rose, & Gordon, 2014).

Crafting a lesson only one way without customizing the options would have negated the genius in him and perhaps left him feeling stupid, disengaged and marginalized from the world of learning that needed him far more than a teacher could have known.

Do you know that there are geniuses still among us today, undiscovered, unchallenged, and unknown? There are geniuses with diagnosis, difficulties and distress waiting for an on-ramp to invite them to the learning. The power to unlock and encourage genius is in your approach to teaching and learning.

Antiracist teachers challenge the key holders to see, acknowledge and pull out the genius of Black and Brown students who society would leave to their own devices to find success. We have a duty to challenge systems to create outcomes that match the belief that skin color should not limit opportunity. Skin color can no longer limit pathways to success.

I love watching the shows about famous people and they share their struggles and failures, but they send love to a teacher who saw something in them before anyone else. I love when a teacher recognized some abstract talent, then opened the door for opportunity with their teaching and feedback. It's the stuff that dreams are made of. Every teacher is a talent scout looking for how they can customize their lessons to unlock geniuses and unleash brilliance in the classroom and in the world.

Reflection

Think about a time when you've seen a skill, talent, or some budding genius in your learning environment.

- What did you do to cultivate it?
- How did you use their natural gifting to enhance their learning experience?

Share with your team.

Resourceful Learners Are Expert Learners

Designing a classroom for students to become expert learners is an essential component of the Universal Design for Learning framework. Students won't become expert learners without coaching and modeling what to do when they come to tasks that are difficult. Using what they know as on-ramps to content they don't know will develop academic perseverance. Expert learners must find and use their resourceful learner muscles. How can you help them work out?

First, emphasize connectivity. Students have to learn to make and verify connections. When they encounter new material, they must learn to connect the dots to prior knowledge, background knowledge, family experiences and or mnemonic devices. This is their opportunity to extend their learning from what they know into what they don't know. Writing in the *New York Times*, Schulten (2017) shares two questions for teachers who are interested in helping students make connections: "First, what is happening in the world that students need to know about and grapple with? Second, how does what's happening in the world connect with the literature, history, civics, science, math and art we know teachers are teaching?"

In her role as editor of The Learning Network, Shulten molds those questions into the shape of activities that help teachers take the guesswork out of making connections for students. Some of the tools that she has helped to craft are Literature Bingo or Picture Prompt series—e.g., "Start with the world and connect it to curriculum," then, "Start with the curriculum and connect it to the world." Once students make connections to themselves, other texts and the world, they will be able to navigate the topic with more authority. The connections will serve as a road map in case they get lost in the learning. They can come back to the last solid connection and begin building again.

Remind students that they should verify and confirm connections because misconceptions are difficult for learning. This is a life skill. Think about how important this is to digital literacy. Researchers found that students commonly displayed a lack of information literacy skills. This highlighted a "weakness as educated consumers of information" and increased the potential for being "easily manipulated" (Eshet-Alkali & Amichai-Hamburger, 2004, p. 426). Before accepting a website, picture, or quote as "truth," before repeating, retweeting, reporting and reposting, expert learners must take a moment to verify the validity of the information. It is the same for all learning. Encourage the connections, and the questions to verify before locking in the link.

Second, turn on the light bulb to information that directly impacts the new learning. On-ramps require a way to map the direction of the learning. Utilizing tools like word sorts, pictures, graphic organizers, movie clips, skits, are all ways to turn the lights on for information that has been stored away. Once the light bulb is on, students will be able to create a context for new information by capturing the learning. Highlighting new information in a way that invites prior knowledge to the party is great. Using tools to capture the light bulb moments seals the learning deal.

The key to learning resourcefully is using the new learning authentically. Students have power. They don't discover the power of that voice until they have the tools to enter the conversation, sustain the conversation, and make a wave in the ocean of learning. Becoming resourceful expert learners is not just about passing standardized tests, which is important, but more so it is about opening the door to lifelong learning that will give students access to worlds that they may have never dreamed of. Resourceful learners are successful people.

When I taught American Literature to a group of 11th-grade students, we studied great American authors. One of the required units was on Emily Dickinson. I know that there are arguments that state that the canon should be discontinued and even other arguments that those white writers should no longer be taught and discussed especially in schools that serve primarily Black and Brown children. I feel that it is important to give Black and Brown students options and a well-rounded literary experience to pair experiences and viewpoints that are different so that learners can form their own.

I wanted students to meet the requirements of the unit and the standards, but beyond that I wanted them to have the confidence and the opportunity to share their brilliance with people in the literary community in a way that solidified their voices, thoughts and analysis skills. Black and Brown children need space to use their resources to build cognitive muscles using a variety of perspectives to challenge the status quo. During our study they had many opportunities to explore her life, her background, her family, her poetry, and other correspondence. Not just her life in isolation but ways that they could relate to her and even things they could not understand about her. Why did she live alone? What's the deal with all the letters? Why did she sew her own books together? Students could choose from webquests, videos, library books, all while using the textbook and required readings to catapult them toward their next level of study. They also made connections from her to readings from other classes, and other authors they loved or despised. The requirements were simply an on-ramp to the learning.

I paired Dickinson's writings with a poem from Langston Hughes. The students looked at both authors word choices, such as capitalization and enjambment. They paired what they had learned about both authors' biographical information with their topics and poetry. They drew some powerful conclusions from their analysis. All of these were on-ramps.

The learning truly happened when some students ventured out into "Emily-land" or "Langston-land" and started posting on scholarly websites, joining forums, even attempting to add to or correct Wikipedia. Some shared their analysis with other English teachers in our school. I loved when a student shared their critical analysis and had to defend their conclusion in the context of a two-way conversation. They read the texts so thoroughly that they found things I wouldn't have even formulated in my wildest dreams. Many students engaged deeply with both Emily and Langston in ways that the textbook or my formal instruction would have never opened the door to. Honestly, the picture of Emily Dickinson that is most widely used doesn't exactly suggest that her poetry will be interesting. But, as the old adage should have said, "Never judge a poet by her picture."

One of the pinnacles for the students was having a scholarly discussion with a professor from a local university. He had authored hundreds of scholarly articles on her and was considered the authority on Emily, as he fondly referred to her. I had taken his course on Dickinson when earning my bachelor's degree, and I knew he was serious about Emily Dickinson when, on the last day of the course, he unbuttoned his shirt to reveal a T-shirt with her picture on it. There was no question about it, this man was smitten.

When he walked into my high-school classroom, he had very little information about what my students would ask him. He knew what poems were in their textbook but had no other preparation for the questions the students would throw at him. The students shared some theories about Dickinson. He questioned them, asked them for the evidence, challenged them to prove their thinking. They quietly huddled to regroup and prepare more questions to get a better handle on their shifting hypothesis. The conversation was rich and deep and challenging. He was thrilled! They were unintimidated by his level of expertise.

Resourceful learning translates to any setting. Black and Brown learners need to know that the tools of learning they are acquiring will set them up for success in any arena, in any audience, with any profession, college or career of their choice. We design learning experiences that allow learners to learn how they learn best and then put it to work. Let them try it out, show it off, think it through, change it up. Multiple means of representation give the learner choices about how to navigate the path to and through the content.

The professor shared a summary statement at the end, "The conversation that we've had today is at a higher level than some of my master's level students. I'm impressed." The bell rang, many students stayed after to argue a few last points and to thank him for his time. Something happened for that group of students. It was an on-ramp.

Can you empower your learners with the resources they need to navigate problems, conversations, debates, and assessments with prowess? They realized that there was value in engaging deeply with literature. When they were questioned or challenged, they leaned on their resourcefulness to push back or rephrase. They found similarities between the little reclusive lady from Amherst and the celebrated hero of the Harlem. Then connections were highlighted when they saw oppression being challenged and opinions being spoken. They found themes emerging and theories formed about being marginalized and having hope for the future. They found out a great truth about themselves and resilience and the power of what they write and what they read and how they correspond. They found legacy wrapped up in a lesson. They found the significance in their own voice, and not necessarily in the right answers, but in the questions.

Being able to volley a hypothesis back and forth with a nationally recognized expert placed them on the road to the expressway of learning. They found themselves learning how to drive toward the destination of their choosing that day. They discovered the power to accelerate learning, decelerate when necessary, pull over and get help, re-enter when you are ready.

They learned the power of the journey and the power of knowing how to use what you have to gain what you don't. They were on the road not because of the scholar in the room, but because they were aware of the tools to use to become the scholar in the room!

Reflection

- How can you empower students to discover, use and embrace resources to empower and monitor their own learning?

- What resources did you use in school to learn and grow? When thinking of those resources what technological advances have been made to enhance each of those methods now?

- Who could you partner with to give your students access to an expert in the field?

- What resources are learners very familiar with? Which ones have they identified or recommended for future students? What do you use to evaluate the effectiveness of resources?

- How do the resources that are available reflect the culture of the learners? What could you do to improve the quality of offerings?

- What on-ramps have you structured for learning? In what area do you need to create more on-ramps?

We respect our students' time and talents by designing lessons that awaken their curiosity, invite their background knowledge, inspire their ingenuity, relate to their real-time dilemmas, and increase their intellectual capacity. Oftentimes we think of multiple means of representation as being paramount at the beginning of a lesson or a unit. We have to shift our approach to reflect a stance of honor by creating multiple on-ramps to the material through the way that our students perceive the material. The ultimate honor for our students is trusting them with the instructional keys to find their own personal learning. This is when learning begins to become deep, wide, interesting, and relevant for students—not just for an assignment but for life.

Action and Expression
Honoring by Releasing

Your classroom is the place where students learn to shine. It is the incubator for thought processes, study skills, and success indicators. It is where students learn and grow because you set the stage for them to learn about themselves and others. Most of all you come away from the stage and allow them the freedom to test out new skills, to make meaning of new content, to utilize resources to make learning sticky for themselves and to share their learning with other learners as well as an authentic audience who will experience the genius you have coached for the big game.

Universal Design for Learning suggests offering learners many ways to show what they know and to tackle assignments and projects. The on-ramps we create using UDL open the road of academic achievement beyond the borders of income, ZIP code, resources, race, class, and gender. No matter where you are, or what you have or what you know—the expressway of learning is available to you.

One time during a practice test, we read an excerpt from Malcolm X's autobiography. Many of the students had heard of him or even perhaps seen Spike Lee's movie about him. But this story focused on the effort that he had put into learning while serving time in prison. He had copied the dictionary, read the newly copied words and their definition aloud to himself, and spent time thinking about the words. He then began reading avidly. He noted that between "my correspondence, my visitors—usually Ella and Reginald—and my reading of books, months passed without my even thinking about being imprisoned. In fact, up to then, I never had been so truly free in my life."

Reading this passage with my students inspired me. I felt inspired by the power of reading and reminded of the realities that not all reading is created equal. How can we also give students the tools to persist, even when they feel the weight of hopelessness and don't know what to do? How can we challenge our assumptions, push our pedagogical boundaries, and expand our preconceived notions of teaching?

I felt a nudge to do something. To try something different. To be something different. To propel my students to different levels, beyond what the state and the state assessments required of them.

I wanted to buck a racist system that had told my students they were not good enough and that they don't have what it takes to succeed. It was just what I needed to rip the bandages off the prescriptive, program-heavy instruction in my classroom and move toward strategies that would not only build a brand of better learners, but also build a better teacher in me and my colleagues.

UDL takes into account the research that says that psychological stressors and restricted access to educational resources are barriers to academic success and couples it with the myriad of scientific research that boasts of the resilience of the brain (Hays, 2015). By giving students options for ways to learn and to show what they have learned, we are honoring their individuality, their backgrounds, and their experience.

Using Dr. Dre to Explain Romeo and Juliet

Honor is an accelerant. It is what jump starts relationships, conversations, trust and interest. Honoring our students means that we are willing to respect their interests and abilities enough to follow their lead when we design opportunities for them to express their learning. It's a lot like Driver's Education. The classroom for Driver's Ed is only tolerated because it leads to the real-world skill. The roadway to a lifetime of driving has two toll booths that everyone must pay. The written portion and the driving portion. There is a guide in the car with you, but they are in the passenger seat and the learner is in the driver's seat. That screams respect. Even if you have never driven a day in your life, the teacher gives you all the space and opportunity in the world to be successful, because even your failures are respected in this environment.

Why is there so much freedom in a driver's education situation? Because all the safeguards are there to keep the student safe. The instructor is within reach to correct the turn of the wheel. Their brake system is attached to yours while you learn your bearings. They use their words to guide you, and the safety systems to protect you, but you do the work. You explore what works for you. You adjust the mirrors. You select how far forward your seat is. You customize your experience and then you put what you know into practice.

Are our classrooms, and the assessments we design, places of honor? Do we allow our students to customize their learning experience as they put the newly learned skills into practice? Do we encourage our students to get out of the parking lot practice of the classroom and get out there in the real world by sharing authentically beyond the classroom—with all of the safety of instruction and the guidance of the brake system of preparation?

We communicate such a respect for them as learners when we allow them to take action and teach. That ownership solidifies that the work they are doing is not, "just for the classroom." Driver's Education is not simply for the sake of knowing how to drive. It is to use those skills to acquire access to the world beyond our walking capacity. Instruction that puts students in the driver's seat expands the possibilities for the improvement of our communities and beyond. Driving regularly in an educational setting empowers the students to build on their learning and transfer that success to other learning environments and, even more importantly, to life.

As a student, I took countless assessments. As you did. Which ones do you remember? I want to share one of mine. The year was 1993. My English teacher, Mrs. Kay, passed out the Romeo and Juliet final projects. She told us that we would have a final test on the unit, but in addition to that we would also have a project. Before she passed the project out she explained that this was a *big deal*, worth a lot of points, and should be taken seriously. I remember feeling excited and nervous because I had fallen in love with Romeo and Juliet, but I was afraid that the project would involve drawing, which I was terrible at, or something that had elements of an art project. I always lost points on those kinds of projects because it was just not my thing.

She passed the papers out, and as I prepared myself for mandatory torture I scanned the sheet. Options? A hand went up in the back of the room. "Do you want us to do all of these?"

"No way," she responded, "Let's go over it together." She then walked us through the assignment choices and I was with her until I landed on, "Write a song or rap from the point of view of one of the characters in the story. Be sure to include some details from each act of the play."

I have no idea what the other options were, but I felt like that option had my name on it. I started writing the lyrics over the weekend and had to come up with a makeshift studio to get my rhymes down. My opening lines, set to the tune of Dr. Dre's,

"Nuthin but a G Thang" instrumental were, "Romeo, Romeo what shall I do/ I'm a Capulet and you're a Montague" I recorded it on a cassette tape and created a typed transcript of my lyrics. My teacher loved it! She graded it, then played it for my class as well. Here is the part that I love.

After that she encouraged me to write for the school literary magazine and to publish my poetry. The project was an on-ramp for her to hear about my goals and share a few potential paths that I knew nothing about. So here I was a young girl, who lived in a neighborhood filled with drug activity, gangs, prostitutes, and abandoned factories dreaming about Shakespeare, creating my own interpretation and introducing my English teacher to *The Chronic* (the album, not the substance).

She was willing to hear from me in my own way, while still requiring me to learn the literary terms and write research papers. She made space for my experience to be relevant to her. Those small gestures helped me to be open to whatever she suggested to me. There is power in honoring the experiences of the students we serve. Let them analyze the lyrics to their favorite songs. Let them find the rhyme scheme in a little gangsta rap. Snag the beats to a few songs on the radio. Learn something different and be open. This is simply an on-ramp that looks differently and sounds differently from anything that you have ever experienced.

In Mrs. Kay's class I didn't feel like I had to change who I was, but I also felt like I wasn't a slave to my neighborhood or my circumstances. I didn't realize it then, but she shaped the kind of teacher that I would later become. She actually lived Universal Design for Learning, and the results were unforgettable! She released the reins of control and allowed us to be authentically ourselves and authentically students of excellence. The sad thing is that this feeling for me was rare. It was one of the first times in my educational career I had a choice. I was in the driver's seat, but I was safe.

Giving students options for how they respond brings about a culture of respect as well. In the afternoon on my way home I sometimes listen to a talk radio show. I am amazed at the multiple means of action and expression that the hosts have created for listeners. When the hosts dive into a topic they often create space for listener input. Calling into a radio show with two lively and debating hosts is seriously daunting, at least to me. I'm always flabbergasted by the number of people who call in and go toe to toe with these guys without a script or the safety net of knowing which side of an issue they actually stand on. What thrills me is that there are multiple ways for listeners to interact. Of course, they can call in, text their comments, leave a comment on a Facebook thread, send a direct Tweet, or comment on the show's Instagram page. Some radio shows even state their mailing address at the end so that folks can still have their say.

Classrooms can be structured to provide options for expression and communication. If I can choose how I participate by either raising my hand, texting in my comments, or adding discussion to a wiki expanding on thoughts or asking questions - then I will find the best way for me to share my input with the class. There are lots of different ways to make sure that everyone has options on how to communicate and participate.

Elevating Action and Expression in a Safe Environment

We can create experiences for students to take action and express what they know in meaningful ways when our classroom and our community is rigorous, reflective, and safe. Students who feel safe are willing to try new things, ask difficult questions and hold each other accountable for protecting that feeling. Classrooms are incubators of hope and sanctuaries of change. Allowing multiple means of action and expression does not mean that the classroom is a "free for all."

Here are a few ideas to consider to create a safe classroom for risk-taking learners as you design opportunities for action, expression, reflection, and learning.

Teach students how to respond to one another

In the same way we teach students acceptable methods to communicate with teachers, we need to be just as intentional about teaching students how to respond to one another. Use sentence starters to promote inquiry. Set standards for how to agree with a classmate's viewpoint. Create guidelines for how to disagree. In this era of social media, opinion vomit is common, expected, and sadly accepted in many circles. Many people quip "I'm entitled to my opinion" while they attack the opinion of another who thinks differently from them. Teaching students how to respond to one another with respect is a dying art that can be revived in your classroom. If you want students to ask questions, take risks, share their uncertainties and expertise then you have to set the stage for all students to be able share and for all students to be able to receive. Novak (2016), an expert in the field of UDL, has an amazing list of sentence starters to help students get in the habit of framing their thoughts in a learning community.

Teach the expectations for effective listening practices

I used to love when my pre-school teacher implored us to, "Put our listening ears on." I always cupped my hands so tightly over my ears that I all could hear was the muffled sound created by the curve of the palm of my hand. I usually missed the directions with my listening ears on. I love the strategies to quiet the room, but they definitely don't equate to listening. Active listening is a skill that requires instructional coaching, practice, feedback, and monitoring. It is also helpful to give students a visual or a tool that will guide them through their interactions. The listening skills that you expect will be more readily evidenced if they are taught, supported, implemented, and celebrated.

Model respectful interactions

Modeling respectful interactions is important especially when promoting risk taking in a classroom. Work together with your class to define what each person expects as respectful interactions. Try your best to give the class some opportunities to come up with what boundaries they expect from other students and from the teacher. This opens the door to share what you expect from students as respectful interactions. Be intentional about explicating when you are modeling an expected behavior. Refresh the expectations often with mini-lessons, songs, skits, poems, discussion, and games. The more the community communicates the expectations clearly to one another, the more likely they are to be met. Communally defining shared expectations around respect will help to shape the community of learners.

Sometimes respect is being communicated by a student but misinterpreted by another student or a teacher. It is important to establish respectful greetings, as far as what name the student wants to be called by or how the teacher would like to be addressed. One of my colleagues was mortified at the fact that most of my students call me Fritz. No Ms. or Mrs.—just Fritz. She had a hard time understanding that we had a mutuality of understanding that allowed us to forego formalities in favor of familiarity but still maintain the respect born out of relationship. We had lots of dialogue, and eventually she understood that my relationship with that particular group of students and her relationship with them was different. One was not better than the other, it was simply different.

We spoke at length about expectations around speaking and using slang and welcoming dialect in the classroom, and this conversation (and a controversy) is ongoing in Black and Brown circles. When we think about the funds of knowledge that students and families have, we have to acknowledge that slang and dialect have rules, usage, grammar, and mechanics just as any language does. Students who can code-switch have an advantage of translingual operation that allows them to navigate differently based on how they perceive the context. Learning standard English is one way of speaking and writing, using dialect is another way.

Antiracist teachers understand that there is more than one way to communicate and they empower learners to understand the nuances and implications of the choice that ultimately rests with them. That is honor. That is power. That is antiracist.

Give opportunities for reflection when expectations are not met

As with any expectation there will be times when members of the learning community fall short, both students and teachers. Plan ahead for these moments and encourage meaningful reflection to promote understanding of what the expectation is, why it was not met and how to meet the expectation in the future. Universal Design for Learning calls for providing appropriate goal setting and support planning and strategy development. When an expectation of the learning community is not me, this is a great time to set some goals and reinforce the development of some personal strategies to help the student exhibit expected behavior.

Create community expectations, rubrics, rewards, and consequences

One way to keep the expectations clear and out in the open is to use rubrics that explain how to meet the expectation and the progression to get back on track if an expectation is not met.

A good rubric also includes some built-in rewards and consequences. These are most effective when the community of learners sets them. Make sure you evaluate each reward and each consequence to make sure it is realistic and beneficial in promoting the desired outcomes. Don't promise a weekly pizza party if you haven't secured the funds to make good on that reward. Ideas for free rewards are available. Spend time with your Professional Learning Community creating a list of free options for celebrations.

Teach peer mediation and leadership principles through your content

When students learn to navigate conflict in a healthy and meaningful manner, they will have more productive academic conversations and interactions. Building a classroom structure that empowers students to work out their conflicts quickly, respectfully and peacefully will benefit the entire learning community by freeing up time to focus on what really matters. Allowing students to pause and think about how the problem or theory can be looked at from different perspectives will help lead them into the principles of mediation. Think about peer leadership and empowering students to take ownership, not just of their own learning, but also their learning environment. Leadership and learning go hand in hand in the ebb and flow of a UDL classroom. A great way to facilitate leadership is to utilize a class meeting structure.

Utilize the class meeting structure regularly

In the book, *Positive Discipline*, Nelson (2006) writes: "The effectiveness of a positive approach depends on adult attitudes of mutual respect and concern for the long-range effects of interactions in the school environment on students" (p. 132). Knowing the impact that adults have on students in the school setting, this structure lends itself to far reaching positivity educationally. Class meetings foster leadership by allowing students to review expectations, set goals and give feedback to each other.

Encourage collaboration over competition

Students love the thrill of playing a game in the classroom. The students who love the game the most are the ones who are good at it and have a natural competitive nature. They live for competition. When structuring a UDL environment, remember that not everyone thrives in a competitive situation. I'm not saying that a good old friendly competition isn't welcome. What I am saying is that it may exclude some students. Collaboration is a powerful skill that enhances the learning of all students. There are many structures that help students benefit from the power of the collective knowledge in the room. Which ones have you tried? Which ones would be a good fit for your classroom?

Use role playing to communicate and solidify expectations

When setting the expectations for a universally designed classroom, students need to explore the nuances of the expectations, rubrics, consequences, and rewards. A great method to help them see variances in what is expected is to role play. Drama gives action to words and insight to the meaning of the words. It also gives students a chance to interpret the expectations and ask questions to clarify misconceptions before moving forward. Historical events that feature an oppressed people group should never be used in role playing experiences. We don't need another generation enacting problematic race relations or oppressive historical events for the sake of perspective or word problem solving. Role play can be used to practice desired outcomes of the standard and rehearse various ways to think through a problem. Listen to your students if they raise an issue. Use your community of practitioners to ask questions to ensure that you are not using intention as a barometer to enact racist practices.

★   ★   ★

All of these structures give ideas for how to build a safe learning community where students feel safe taking risks in taking action and expressing their learning. Make sure that students have ample opportunities for practicing these skills. Build in time to intentionally discuss and reflect on the implementation of the practices that build community. Build in time for practice and participation. When the elements are in place that allow for safe sharing of ideas, respectful exchange of opinions, mutual collaboration and clearly communicated expectations it opens the door for a powerful hub of teaching and learning to emerge.

A Word about Standardized Tests

One silver lining of the COVID-19 shutdown in 2020 was that most states and districts cancelled end-of-year standardized tests—and the weeks of prep that go with them. Of course, standardized testing is a gargantuan elephant in the room anytime education is discussed. The tests measure certain skills that don't always showcase the student's greatest strength or give support for their weaknesses. And the reality is that closing the black-white achievement gap is "disappointingly slow" (Camera, 2016).

The Coleman (1966) Report mandated by the Civil Rights Act of 1964 examined the differences in standardized outcomes between Black and white students. The results are sobering. According to Camera (2016), "The Coleman Report found, among many other things, that in both math and reading the average Black student in grade 12 placed in the 13th percentile of the score distribution, meaning that 87 percent of white students in grade 12 scored ahead of the average Black 12th grader." Today, more than 50 years later, the average Black 12th-grader placed only in the 19th percentile in math and 22nd percentile in ELA (Camera, 2016). Clearly something is not working. For decades, advocates for Black and Brown student have pointed to cultural and racist bias in these tests as evidence that they are part of a rigged system.

Standardized tests offer only a minimum measure of student success. Most of us have no control over the questions, the format, or the structure of these assessment systems. They are predetermined for our students to meet on the designated day of testing. While testing is rigid and legislatively necessary, it does not dictate how we prepare our students.

Even though drivers may have practiced all the necessary skills, they cannot be licensed until they are assessed. No matter how daunting that assessment is, it is necessary to obtain the permits to drive legally. The test has parameters, rules, and point systems that are a state minimum of what you need to know to be able to drive. Once you take and pass the test, you don't stop learning—though technically you could. You keep learning how to drive in varied weather conditions, you learn how to navigate parking spaces instead of orange cones. You also learn to navigate the nuances of traffic with drivers at various skill levels and awareness. None of these variables are tested to obtain your license, but it is a system in which, by practice, we all continue to learn and grow.

As teachers and leaders of schools that serve Black and Brown students we have to remember that we send messages to our students on a regular basis—whether intentional or unintentional. Many state assessment systems check in on students once a year and send back a very clear message. "You are a failure." Or for some students they get the message, "You passed the test, but your school is a failure." And for others, "Your school is passing but your district is a failure." There have been many studies that prove that achievement on standardized tests is directly related to socioeconomic status and race (Hays, 2015).

Assessment systems that send negative messages and require mandatory participation year after year trap students and teachers in a cycle of hopelessness. The message that is loud and clear is, "You are Black, poor or disadvantaged, so you are a failure. But we expect you to perform better, or you will be in trouble." Crippling pressure!

The weight of mandatory testing is carried on the students' shoulders year after year. Sundry other mandates pepper their school experience but very few messages honor them and their abilities and their interests and their backgrounds. I can't think of one state assessment that speaks of situations where street credibility would actually be an asset. Wouldn't that be awesome if the questions gave Black and urban students the upper hand for once?

That said, standardized testing is unlikely to go away any time soon, and it is a hurdle every successful learner will have to get over. So while we can work together to advocate against using standardized tests for accountability, promotion, college entrance, and scholarships, we still need to teach our students to navigate these tests—like drivers need to learn to successfully enter and exit dangerous roundabouts. Our students have to become resilient. Resilience does not mean waiting to fail in order to bounce back. It means preparing to the path to success with support, receiving feedback, receiving the invitation to display genius, shining in the way that you are created to, being celebrated for the way you shine, then transferring your brilliance in many ways so that world will know you've been licensed to drive on the expressway to success.

Failure as Feedback for Excellence

I'm a recovering perfectionist. Even in recovery, I have a hard time undoing the years of training that have taught me that, "Practice makes perfect." So many projects that were given to me in my formal schooling led me to pursue a grade, and not an idea or the learning. The pursuit of knowledge was hardly ever sparked by assignments. I was on the hunt for an A.

A is for agony.

Here is the cycle. Get the assignment. Size up the instructor's standards. Do exactly what they asked of me. Get the grade. Forget the content. Learn nothing. Ugh!

Now that I'm an educator, I want to change my A from agony to Audri!

Audri is a 7-year-old boy who dreams of becoming a theoretical physicist. He has already decided that he wants to go to MIT and study robotics. This kid dreams big. I admire the big dreams, but what I admire even more is Audri's drive to persevere in the face of failure. In his viral YouTube video, Audri records attempt after attempt of his Rube Goldberg machine (Littlepythagoras, 2012). A Rube Goldberg machine is a contraption that consists of many complicated chain reactions to achieve a simple outcome. Audri rigged a series of dominos to push down the switch on a surge protector, which activated a toaster, that popped up a lever, that released a roll of paper, that set off a paper towel tube, that knocked over a wine glass, that released a pulley, that revealed an upside down silver bowl that came down over the top of a stuffed animal that Audri dubbed a monster. His imagination and perseverance were evident as Audri recorded his hypothesis of how many failures he would experience before he got to success. He guessed that he would fail up to 20 times before he got things just right. More amazing that his imagination was his positivity matched with perseverance. This kid literally danced through each attempt even when it ended in failure. You could hear an adult in the video who was just excited about the machine and he was.

Audri expected to fail, but he didn't waste the failure. He used the failures to learn how to succeed. Failure is feedback—if you gather information to be more successful the next time. After only three failures Audri met success on his fourth run. He embraced failure, then squeezed the juice of success out of each run. At the end of the video he shares the age-old wisdom that, "If at first you don't succeed—try, try again." Audri has taught me that failure is golden!

The failure that I have been afraid of and running from for all of my academic career has been trying to teach me what Audri has learned at a really young age! Chris Sturgis (2017), co-founder of CompetencyWorks, urges teachers "to build a culture of reflection as they stretch themselves to strengthen their understanding of their tasks as leaders . . ." In other words, teachers need a growth mindset.

I think what Chris is saying is that Audri would not reach success if he wasn't surrounded by a community that taught him how safe and productive it is to fail. We have to build that in school communities in order to reach "Destination Success" while parked on the corner of hope and fear. This is the power of feedback. How do we prepare our students to learn from their failures? How do we, ourselves, learn from failure? Are we dancing at the prospect of what our mistakes reveal, or fretting over falling short of the impossible goal of perfection.

Yes, in the age of high stakes testing and accountability we have an obligation to introduce learning communities to the power of failure. Nico Pitney (2015) puts it this way: "A parent gives the gift of failure by thinking in the long-term rather than in the short-term; by thinking less about checking off the imaginary box—'Was I a good parent today?'—and thinking more about 'Was I a good parent this year?'" (p. 4)

Parent. Teacher. Leader.

Reflection

- In my role, have I enlarged my expectations of learning by creating safe places to fail—to learn—to grow?

- How do my students or colleagues view failure? What small thing can you do to help them see failure as a gift?

You don't have to be perfect to achieve greatness. Perseverance is learned on the footpath of mistakes! Audri gets it! I'm learning this! Where are you on this journey? College counselor and writer Brennan Barnard (2017) asks, "What is the antidote to the societal messages that adolescents receive about aiming high, self-confidence, creativity, disappointment and humility? Failure—it is time to embrace and reframe failure, not as catastrophe, but rather as opportunity. Not as devastation, but rather as healthy deviation."

Failure is healthy. When this becomes a normalcy and not an anomaly then we will see innovation and resilience and passion and achievement. Chasing success without embracing failure leaves us robotic, empty, checking boxes and bubbling circles. Audri kept track of his failures. He didn't mope about them. He celebrated the success in each failure. He documented her journey. He shared his learning. I asked myself, "What does his classroom look like?" "How does his teacher model failure?" "How does his principal celebrate success." Embracing failure doesn't happen by accident! It is an intentional set of practices steeped in the belief that each set back is teaching me something that I can use in the future. We can create that space for our students. As a community of learners, we can model that grace and learn from our failures right alongside them. Failure is teaching and learning. And, finally, after all these years, I'm learning from failure. Failure is earning an A! The difference between failing downward and failing forward is feedback. Consider Audri. Without some kind of feedback, he would have continued to practice the same run over and over again with no adjustments.

Without adjustments there is no learning and no point at all to success or to failure. Feedback richens the learning process. Instructional designers Holly Fiock and Heather Garcia (2019) suggest four ways to make sure feedback is effective:

1. Affirm what students do well, giving them a springboard to build a foundation of success.

2. Share correction and direction to give students an idea of where they went wrong and information about how to get back on track.

3. Emphasize that process is the "squeeze" that allows lemons to become lemonade. Without pointing out the process the good stuff of failure goes to waste.

4. Coach students to critique their own efforts. This gives them the ammunition to learn powerful lessons for themselves and apply that perseverance to the lesson at hand and those that will come in the future.

Feedback increases learning because it creates expert learners who know where they are on the road to their goal and what they need to do to get there. Without feedback a student who is off track will have no idea how to get back on track, and even worse, they may not have any idea they are lost.

Feedback really helped me to gain the knowledge I needed to pass the driver's exam. Though I had taken driving courses at 16 to get my license, I didn't have the opportunity to get the driving practice needed to successfully attempt the driving portion of the exam. At the age of 19, I went back for lessons. decided that I needed to get a license. My driving teacher, Mrs. Foote, was a very stern, older Black woman. The first time I met her, she established a few ground rules before we took off. She went over the normal safety precautions: seatbelt, mirrors, the tandem braking system. But the last one was most important. "I will be teaching as you are driving. When we pull over intermittently, I will give you feedback. You need to listen!" Her tone was already scolding. "You are a little older than the drivers I normally have, but I will make sure you get what you need so that you can be SAFE on the road. Do you understand me?"

She set the environment in her own way to make sure that I understood that her feedback was not for fun, but it was for me to get to my end goal. Her feedback was a shortcut between my lack of experience and reaching my ultimate goal—not just to get a license, but to be a *safe* driver. I felt a sense of shame at first because I was probably one of very few students in my college dorm that did not know how to drive. I felt embarrassed when she had to pick me up and I was unsure if I would ever become a good driver because I was so far behind. Her approach honored my position, but also gave me a roadmap toward the overarching goal. She honored my fear by inviting me toward success—but with conditions. I needed to listen to, understand and apply the lessons from her feedback.

What can students do with your feedback? Are you framing it in a way honors the learners fears, anxieties, and maybe even misconceptions? Honoring students wherever they are on the expressway to success means that the instruction reminds them of their overarching life goals. We have to honor what they want to do or the road they ultimately want to travel, even if that road is simply discovering their interests more fully. We honor that by sharing quality feedback to remove doubt about what steps it would take for the learner to overcome their challenges in order to meet their goal.

What is quality feedback? At its core, quality feedback is simply external information that lets a person know where they are in relation to their goal and what steps are still remaining to get there. Much like a GPS system, there must be ongoing opportunities for two-way dialogue.

When a destination is clear and you type that exact address into the GPS system, it first looks at where you are before giving you directions on how to get there. There are also a few customization questions so that the best route for you is clear: are you driving, walking, biking, or taking the bus. After you give your answers, there are choices available to further customize your route—avoid tolls, avoid expressways, take a specific street and other choices to get you to your destination in a way that is good for you. My favorite part of consulting a GPS is that often you will know if there is traffic or an accident that will slow you down.

The GPS will then follow along with you, giving you feedback on the next steps to take along your route. In the event you get off track, with even something so simple as a wrong turn, you will hear feedback: Recalculating! That feedback will then create a plan for course correction that takes you either back to the original path or customizes another set of directions in order for you to make it to your destination. When you reach your desired destination, the GPS celebrates that "You have arrived!" by announcing your accomplishment.

After you have arrived there is sometimes an opportunity for you to rate the route so that the manufacturer or web developers will know if this route was accurate, helpful and/or correct. GPS systems are such a popular form of guidance and feedback that they are accessible in various formats. Some are separate devices, others are merged into devices that like cell phones, still others are built into the cars. To be most effective these technologically advanced devices depend on the feedback of users to get ready. The users depend on the feedback of the system to be accurate. The one proven benefit of the system is that the destination is reached!

Educators are the GPS system for students. They don't have to know exactly what career field they are interested in or what postsecondary options they will choose in order to receive direction toward a destination. Often when I am in need of guidance to a destination, I simply type in an intersection or a monument in the area where I want to go. The GPS gives me general guidance to help me figure things out along the way.

Educators get to develop that sense of direction with students, so that the route toward success looks familiar to them as they travel. Feedback to students does not mean that we tell them where they want to go, but rather we take in information to customize a path of direction for learning with them. Racism in action removes this power from learners. We tell them what they should strive for and then tell them how to get there.

Antiracist UDL empowers learners to make choices for their own destination. We have to listen to their goals, their plans, or their lack of specificity and then work with them to customize learning experiences that give them a sense of their current location in relation to the learning standards and the turns it will take for them to reach either a specific destination or a general area of personalized success. We have no right to overshadow the voice of a learner with our desires for their lives. They get to drive to the destination of their choice. We get to help them think through the power of their choices and coach them toward developing the muscle of independence. If the option they choose does not work, they will have a plan of resilience that builds them dually.

When there are misconceptions, habits and/or bad decisions that will slow them down, or threaten to take them off the desired route, we must be instrumental in announcing that recalculating is not a bad thing and not a put down, but simply a mutual commitment to the destination. Our students need to know that we want them to make it to their desired outcome— not by happenstance but by calculating what it takes to get there and then following the turn by turn steps and enjoying the journey.

Feedback is mutually beneficial. Traveling a new route is scary, at least for me. There have been times when the GPS has suggested twists and turns that I thought were beneficial, until I realized that it took me away from where I really wanted to go. There were other times, when I ditched the route and ended up at a road closure or stuck on a one-way street going the wrong way. Students have the power of choice, even when the feedback is prescriptive and specific.

The Mutual Benefits of Feedback

When we share routes, options, and customization possibilities with students, we must be diligent to check in with them. Receiving feedback on our instruction means asking questions like, "Which option works best for you?" When using a GPS we make decisions like, would I like the voice directions on or off, do I want only the next turn visible or do I want the whole route. Is it better for me to use my phone, or do I want to print it ahead of time just in case I lose reception or my battery dies.

A student may not necessarily think about these customizations in terms of the lesson, but we get to help them see this on their journey. Try all the supports and keep the settings that best meet your needs. In your teaching, what supports have you introduced to students? What devices, extensions, or web sites have been helpful in having students chart progress to their destination? Do you use visual aids to help them see progress? Do you record your feedback for auditory learners? When sharing feedback with students, do they have a mechanism to respond? How often are students capturing what supports are helpful to them? Are you checking in with students to find out what teaching methods are helpful? Do they have the option of giving you feedback on your teaching?

Feedback is mutually beneficial when it helps both parties achieve the desired purpose. The feedback that you give today makes customizing the next excursion more accessible and more accurate for all travelers. The same is true in urban education. We don't have to reinvent the wheel, but we do have to realize that the same tires won't work for every vehicle. Customization of the route toward a student's destination is honoring both their destination and their journey. It is a high level of respect because your actions give them resources for today and information for tomorrow.

Whether you are putting multiple methods in place for students to respond or empowering them with tools to express themselves with multimedia or simply helping them to choose a goal and monitor their progress, you are giving them the tools to grow and develop as learners. The most effective learners know that the floor of knowledge is as deep as the ceiling is high. Both are limitless. Expert learners know that failure is never final, and neither is the thrill of success. Each feat will serve the learner as they squeeze the learning out of failure and build on the foundation of success. Just as drivers don't arrive at one location and park in one spot forever—learners don't set a goal and park on that spot never intended to learn again.

Customizing the journey of learning is documented by giving and receiving feedback in these six areas.

1. **Destination.** At the onset of every journey the destination has to be determined. It is also important to make sure along the way that the destination is clear, and mutually agreed upon. Nothing is more frustrating than moving in the same direction only to find out that the end result I want differs from the end result you want. It is important for teachers to provide opportunities for students to express their career destination or interests. The destination does not have to be an overall decision, but rather simply a learning goal, skill acquisition, myth busting or deciding on a road to travel. Whatever it is, be clear on a destination to help guide the learning experiences along the way.

2. **Customization.** After an established destination, utilize the information to customize next steps. Customization is simply tailoring the learning experiences for students who have similar interests, learning styles, goals and/or destinations. Plan to guide their journey so that they can merge together and glean what they need while staying true to their original destination. While they journey together customize experiences that will consistently answer the question what's in it for me.

3. **Calibration.** Every student should always understand the why behind their learning. The answer to the why should never be for a grade, or because the teacher told me to. Calibration is a check in that clarifies learning expectations and contexts for the learning experiences. Where does this fit in the real world, and in the journey toward their goal, and on the grand prize of life goals.

4. **Mobilization.** Having an idea of where the learning fits is one thing, but test driving your learning in the real world is a totally different ball game. How will students prepare for

interactions with an authentic audience of professionals in the field? What opportunities or connections will I bring into the classroom for my students to be mobilized into interacting with, bouncing ideas off and learning from an authentic audience of professionals.

5. **Recalculation.** Create opportunities for reflection and new learning goals after mobilizing activities. Think about ways for students to share what they have learned, or craft new questions or destinations after being mobilized outside of the student-teacher/ peer learning community.

6. **Celebration.** Even if students have more questions, a new destination or a less than pleasant experience make sure there is room to celebrate. As you forge ahead with a UDL atmosphere in your classroom the feedback loop will be continuous. As you ask questions and as your students search for answers while creating questions always make room to celebrate! What does celebration look like? It simply means positively locking in the learning with an experience that captures the essence of what has taken place. How to celebrate may be something you brainstorm while in the destination phase.

This journey is not just for the students. It is a joint journey that places the teacher in the passenger seat at times and allows the student to drive. The students will receive feedback and guidance from you. You will receive feedback and guidance from the student. It's frightening and exhilarating all at the same time, but the goal is to get to a destination and celebrate. Everyone will be able to celebrate something! Who doesn't enjoy a celebration?

Constructing a Universally Designed, Antiracist Classroom

Construction zones are not beautiful, but the outcome often is. No one loves orange barrels on the expressway. Everyone loves the two-lane headache that has emerged into a four-lane butterfly after construction. Construction is the price we pay for a smooth commute free of traffic jams and obstructions. Anyone who has lived in a major metropolitan city knows that when one construction project comes to an end another one emerges. Something is *always* under construction.

Building a community of learners is messy. Launching into community building with the lens of antiracism is even messier. The moment race is interjected there are defenses that go up and old experiences that come up. The word is loaded with a bitter history and there is no clean, clear cut way to attack and dismantle systems that were designed for white people to win. Though antiracist work is messy it is worth it. There is always the dust of old mindsets, and the jackhammer of common challenges that threaten every school's attempt at reform. Real change is never pretty, but it is worth it. Building right in the midst of the mess is always worth the beauty that follows.

Equitable systems will emerge that tear down walls of division and open doors of success for all. The beauty of one light bulb coming on. The beauty of a blog or video of your students showcasing their learning going viral. The beauty of seeing the confidence grow, or convincing a skeptical teacher to try something new, or admitting that you don't know to a student who is becoming an expert learner. There is beauty when a teacher throws an assignment out that she did each year because she recognizes how offensive it can be for Black or Brown students. Every time you see an orange barrel on the expressway, I'm sure it doesn't evoke a warm and fuzzy response. But maybe it's time for that attitude to change. The only time you see an orange barrel is when there is change coming. Normally it's not just any change—it is change for the better.

Currently an expressway that my family travels often has gone from four lanes to two. This change has been a test of our patience to say the least. Even on Sundays this change brings massive slow-downs and a barrage of brake lights. It's awful! I have to force myself to remember three important things: 1) The work is being done to create a safe structure; 2) It won't always be this way; and 3) It will be better when the work is done.

Those three thoughts don't exactly evoke joy when I see the signs that say, "Construction Zone Ahead." I don't cheer out loud when I see the orange barrels, the cones, the flashing lights, or the workers. I don't exactly feel overwhelmed with a sense of contentment to be inconvenienced and slowed down when all I want to do is hit the pedal and get to my destination. Nope! This is not my initial response. Yours either? I'm glad I'm not alone.

The construction zone is daunting for drivers even if the end-result is for our own benefit. I want to pause to look at the construction zone of UDL when informed by antiracist work and pull a few safety tips for each of us no matter where we are on our road of implementation.

Construction zones often require gear to ensure that workers and onlookers are safe. Building a UDL environment is risky. Sure, there are plenty of potential dangers, but also plenty of potential benefits. New drivers and experienced drivers alike should be extra cautious in a construction zone, but that does not mean that any of us are actually cautious. On the UDL journey, especially when working with Black and Brown students, there are some implementation signs you can look for to ensure that you avoid the danger of burnout and diminish the temptation of giving up.

Whether you have been implementing Universal Design for Learning for many years or if the principles in the framework are brand new, you are definitely entering into a construction zone of learning. This is especially true if this is the first time you are doing this work through an antiracist lens. Because this work is constantly tearing down barriers and building on-ramps there is some danger involved. Remember the three attitude adjusting thoughts about construction that I mentioned? Consider them when you are gearing up for action:

1. Universally designed lessons will make your class safer for learning for all students, especially your Black and Brown students.

2. While implementation has times where it can be super messy, inconvenient and nerve wrecking—with practice and reflection—it won't always be this way.

3. It will all be worth it when you arrive at your work's purpose each time you eliminate barriers for the students you serve. It will all be worth it. You know the risks of having students fall through the cracks.

Your Personal Protective Equipment

I first began to create this analogy of personal protective equipment (PPE) before the COVID-19 pandemic, but now I can't read it without thinking of the disparities that COVID exposed for the Black and Brown communities. The Center for Disease Control (2020) reported that death rates among Black/African American persons (92.3 deaths per 100,000 population) and Hispanic/Latino persons (74.3) were substantially higher than those of white (45.2) or Asian (34.5) persons. This provides yet more evidence that our systems are not inequitable, and that racism is deep within our American institutions.

While we have all become more acquainted with PPE to protect ourselves from killer virus, we are still in danger of the killer of racism and the impact that it has on disproportionate outcomes for Black and Brown students. Are we ready to put on some educational PPE to ensure that the environments will be safe for students who, just by entering the doors of the school are at risk. The data shows that Black and Brown students are in the danger zone in our schools.

As you prepare to serve these brilliant minds, check your gear to make sure you are ready for action in the construction zone.

Hard hats

Hard hats are a must in a construction zone. They protect your head and skull in the event that heavy equipment or pieces of material fall down. Why do you need your hard hat for antiracist UDL implementation? This work takes strategic planning and thinking for long-term and short-term success. A very dangerous approach to this work is believing that creativity and spontaneity are the enemy of planning and strategizing. An antiracist UDL classroom is flexible and forward thinking, but it is also steeped in intentionality backed by action and preparation. Planning and utilizing the UDL lesson tools is protection for construction zones moving toward the goal of building expert learners. Planning and checking the plans to ensure that the classroom is not a hazard zone for Black and Brown students is the protective gear that keeps the focus on the outcome instead of shifting the focus to careless accidents that may detract from learning instead of spurring it on. If Black and Brown students are failing to meet the standard and there is not a relational safety emerging, then I am creating hazardous conditions where no one is safe.

Safety glasses

Protecting your vision is of the utmost importance in a construction site. It sounds like a no brainer, but protective eyewear is tricky. You have to be able to have unrestricted vision, but still protect your eyes in the process. Eye wear comes in various forms but depending on the work you are doing the protective eye gear changes. When it comes to selecting antiracist UDL eye protection there are a few things to keep in mind:

- Select eyewear that protects against specific hazards. Wearing a welding mask to a chemistry lab wouldn't provide the correct kind of protection and you would also get lots of funny looks. In terms of antiracist UDL, what have you seen that has excited you about this work? Is it informed by Black and Brown viewpoints? What can you do to see more of it? Early in implementation you may not have many practical examples of work that is explicitly antiracist and UDL for you to view in person on a regular basis. In this work, you become the army, linking together resources until we create a community that is committed to implementing for outcomes. The beauty of UDL is that there are videos and implementation communities for you to connect with via the internet and social media to keep your vision fresh and even those communities need a challenge to embrace antiracist practices.

• Eyewear should be durable and cleanable. Construction zones are not productive if they don't get messy. Messy means progress. Your protective gear may get stained or dinged or dented. Keep in mind that is the purpose. In UDL implementation you will try teaching strategies and learning episodes that are inevitably risky and messy and all over the place. The protection is in place for you to take a step back, dust off, make adjustments, and head right back into the construction zone. If at any time in antiracist work we develop a mindset that says there is only one way to see the issues of racism or only one ways to solve them, then that is a surefire sign our lenses are covered and we are NOT seeing clearly. Durability of your gear makes you an effective builder! Your protective gear keeps you from being afraid or resistant. You can take a risk and remain safe. You can see the construction zone but maintain a picture of the finished product. It is possible to be covered in mess and muck, but still plan for greatness. We have to have eyewear that we can clean off, that we can constantly check the lenses to know whether we are seeing clearly, or if we have adjusted to dirty goggles over time. Check your lens often to say clear on the work and the mission.

High-visibility safety vest

In high traffic areas construction workers would be ridiculously unsafe if they blended in with the background and looked like a part of the building or the grounds. The brightly colored vests alert onlookers that a different kind of work is happening here. The vest causes drivers to proceed with caution and keeps the worker from being run over by drivers who are barreling forward on their own mission. If there is one piece of gear that I could require every antiracist UDL seeker, experimenter, convert and expert to wear it would be the brightly colored vest. To implement antiracist Universal Design for Learning and maintain safety, you need to come out of the shadows and the background and let people know that you are trying standing for a change that is necessary! It may not be popular. It may be misunderstood. The vest is not a badge of pride, nor is it a cloak of shame. It simply alerts others that the work I am doing is messy and dangerous, but beneficial at the same time.

The vest lets others know who are interested in the work, that there is a community of committed educators that are willing to do something different to bring different results for Black and Brown students. This is my appeal. This piece of gear is for safety that comes with creating an antiracist and universally designed community. It is impossible to hide in the background. It is impossible to do this work and blend in. It is impossible to be a practicing activist and escape criticism. It is impossible to be antiracist behind closed doors without fighting for every door to be kicked down that holds Black and Brown students back. Put on the vest, look for other vests and recognize that the hard work and heart work will yield results for generations.

Hearing protection

Invite questions but shield your ears from the naysayers and those who are negative about the power of this work. Shield your ears from the voices of white privilege that seek to interrupt our advocacy by saying, "All lives matter." Not another moment can be spent tending to those who seek to hijack the message that injustice against Black and Brown people has to stop. As educators, we have influence. We have power. We have a choice.

Your job is not to convert teachers but rather to join forces with teachers who are serious about designing powerful learning experiences that invite Black and Brown voices to the very tables they have been marginalized from for both learning and teaching. Universal Design for Learning will be approached differently by different people, different systems, and different districts but we must address racism as we empower with voice and choice. There is certainly room for flexibility and adaptability, but there is no room for mistaking that there is racial injustice happening every single day all around the world based on skin color. There are many skeptics, and honestly the skeptics are welcomed to spend time with the most current research and come to the same conclusion that the system is unjust, inequitable and favors whiteness. There is a dire need for antiracist UDL applications for our Black and Brown students.

We have to protect our ears from words and opinions that diminish our personal fire to implement. This will be different for each person. The "what" of UDL is always up for discussion. It has to be in order to foster collaborative communities that push all students toward the success they deserve. The "why" of UDL can be discussed, but don't allow anyone to push you out of your why. Black lives matter is my why! Brown lives matter is my why! UDL is a potentially powerful tool for social justice and antiracism in our schools.

When people ask why we do this work, introduce them to the danger of what happens when we do not. Consider this your permission slip to stand on a soap box and preach about injustice and exclusion. If you need a little assistance determining if it's time for hearing protection, ask yourself the following questions:

- Is this professional conversation assisting me with the goal of ensuring that Black and Brown students are learning?

- Is this professional conversation giving me an additional dose of motivation to propel me forward when my work is toughest?

- Is this professional conversation arming me with examples of how the students I serve are thriving in another environment in the school?

- Am I learning about strategies, interventions, or technological tools that could eliminate barriers for Black and Brown learners?

If the answer to any or all of the questions is no, then use your refusal strategies to move the conversation forward. This is not always easy or even possible.

It is also important to safeguard yourself against the pitfall of discouragement. Implementation of antiracist Universal Design for Learning takes time and courage. There is a vast body of research on antiracism and a plethora of examples of UDL to learn from but very seldom are these two schools of action (not just schools of thought) put together. Thinking that this framework will instantly change every Black or Brown learner in your presence is a myth at best. Antiracist UDL is an expressway to learning. Even traveling on the expressway does not get you to your destination instantly. Even when we fly to our destination, we don't teleport there in an instant (not yet at least, according to my 12-year-old).

Instant transformation is not the goal of antiracist UDL. Crafting a journey that every Black and Brown member of your learning community can fully engage in and learn from is the goal. It is possible. You will get there. We will get there.

The Personal Protective Gear for this antiracist UDL journey will only serve as your safety belt if you choose to buckle up. I can't guarantee there won't be bumps and bruises along the way. I can almost guarantee you that there will be, but this equipment is meant to keep you safe from giving up on the work that our Black and Brown students so desperately need from you. It is to protect the vision words and the deeds and the seeds that you are building, protecting, and planting. This section is to remind you that the work we do is communally beneficial, and that community of learners includes YOU! You have a chosen to lead by choosing to learn about antiracist Universal Design for Learning. The worst tragedies are those that could have been prevented. I want your

hope and your joy and your time and your effectiveness to be celebrated and protected. Let's get your gear ready for action.

Reflection

- When did you make the decision to enter the UDL construction zone?

- When did you make the decision to enter the antiracism construction zone?

- What personal protective equipment do you need to sustain you on your journey to universally design your classroom and become an antiracist educator?

- What practices do you have in place to ensure that you have an adequate balance of dream time and grind time?

Finding Your Teaching Tribe

No matter what level of expertise you feel that you have accom-
plished in implementing antiracist UDL, there is always a great
deal to learn. Socrates said, "I know one thing: that I know nothing." He is known for his wisdom, but he humbly surrendered his
wisdom to remain a student. In the implementation of antiracist
UDL, we have to do the same thing. Yes, we will have great successes and outstanding accomplishments. Some of them will
be secret and some of them will be public, but the one thing we
will need is community. It is important that we continue to find
communities where we feel like a novice. We have to surround
ourselves with brain bursting rock stars that give us heights to
aspire to, crazy inspiration to try new things and stories of success that motivate us to reach those students who are far away
from their own goals.

Although there is no silver bullet there is a vast body of research and wisdom for us to pull from in order to bring about change that we can be proud of when the dust clears. The word change in schools that serve Black and Brown students can be laughable. I remember early in my teaching career I mentioned that I wanted to be a change agent to a veteran teacher. She laughed so hard while glancing up into my wide eyes between her fits of fancy. Her words to me were startling, "She said every few years everything changes, and if you stick around long enough whatever they throw away will come back again." She had given up on change. She didn't believe she could drive change. She felt that she was a victim to it. This belief that, "It is what it is until they tell us what it is now," is scary, but it does not have to prevail. She was one teacher who had thirty years of experiences to support her assertions, and in her own way she was just trying to arm me for the best chance at success in an urban school.

My preservice teacher program was focused on success in urban schools and three principles that our entire master's program was built around were resistance, persistence, and resilience. I didn't know I would have to use all three within my first few days of teaching. In those early days I found a power tribe that was an army of sorts. One was a Social Studies teacher, one was a Spanish teacher, and the third taught students with disabilities in a self-contained setting. These women got a hold of me and gave me quick feedback, let me cry in their rooms after a disaster lesson, pushed me to try the ideas I was sure would fail, and inspired me by incorporating some of my ideas into their courses. A tribe had found me!

Research by Goddard, Hoy, and Hoy (2004) defined collective efficacy as: "The group members' shared perception or belief that they can dramatically enhance the effectiveness of an organization. The collective efficacy of the teachers in a school is a better predictor of student success in schools than is the socioeconomic status of the students." A tribe of teachers found me who believed we could teach the 99% Black student population of students even if they learned differently. They were teachers who not only believed in change or preached about change—but lived it so deeply in their educational practice that their passion was contagious. I took some risks and asked them questions, share lessons with them. I used my planning period and even sometimes used my lunch period to watch them teach and ask them about pedagogical decision making. All three women were very different in their approach but believed deeply in changing their teaching to meet the needs of students.

I observed a Street Law course where students had created a government-like structure within the classroom to explicate the branches of our current government. The classroom management system was set up to deepen their understanding of the standards for the course. Each student received quality attention from the teacher, who shared the burden for teaching, reteaching, collaborating, and assessing with the entire class. I was amazed. Students were not just engaged, but they also translated their learning to the required assessment. Many of her students volunteered their time to participate in the Mock Trial program, the School Court program, and many other civic themed activities. She used music, videos, art, seating, props, decorations, and everything in the room to drive home the standards for students in different ways. She was masterful at creating an environment that served the needs of the students first. She made herself available to me and any other teachers that wanted to work together. She is a phenomenal woman and she taught me the power of collective efficacy. Though we taught in one of the poorest cities in Ohio, that had all the challenges that urban areas bring—drugs, gangs, guns, you name it—we believed together that our students, then and now are worth the very best education we could give to them. If it meant our room was a mess, or our methods were obscure, or that traditionalists would scoff at our attempts, sneer at our successes and laugh heartily at our failures—it was worth it. Have you found your people? Have you been laughing at them? It doesn't matter what you've thought in the past, find them. Connect with them. Make a difference for the students they are reaching by allowing them to reach you too.

Empowering Your Students to Drive Their Learning

Teaching in an urban area, or teaching brilliant Black or Brown students, means you have to do some mechanical work. A car can be beautifully painted on the outside with spinning rims and shiny chrome, but if you never look under the hood you will never know if it is a prize. In the same way when you see a car with scratches and dents, and all kinds of rust on the outside, you may be surprised to find a powerful engine with lots of life left when you crank that baby up. It's the same in education.

You are a mechanic who gets the joy of looking beyond what you see. You get to ignore the noise of stereotypes, look past the squeaky wheel of standardized testing, and give attention when the check engine light is on. You are the key and the catalyst. You diagnose which system is in need of attention. You rally assistance when needed. You do whatever it takes to get that puppy rolling again. Remember when you started teaching, you imagined hearing the roar of the engine when a student was ignited by learning something new. You longed to see the open-door light flip on and when it did you knew that the battery was working. Antiracist UDL practices hand the keys over to the students. You get to coach them and guide them as they start up their engines. You give them the fuel that they need to accelerate, then you watch them as they place their hands at 10 and 2 and merge out of the safe lane to the on-ramp of success.

You have some idea where they are going. You've armed them with tools and tricks to navigate both standstills and

70-mile-an-hour traffic. They know how to pull over and ask for assistance. They have mastered using what they know to gain what they don't. Even though they are sailing, now while you can see them, they are aware that there are potholes, pitfalls, danger signs, and warnings. They know what to do, and how to do it, but yet are keenly aware that on this journey they couldn't possibly know everything that they will face. You smile knowing you have empowered a driver to make it to the next city over, or over to the other coast of the country. You taught them to drive, to take control of their learning. You've taught them how to navigate systems that have judged the ability of their vehicle just by looking. You gave them the keys and the freedom to access, accelerate and advance toward their personal and educational goals despite whether society thinks they belong.

They are driving now on the expressway to success because you chose to inspire greatness beyond location, beyond circumstance, beyond impossibility and beyond race. Greatness is not tied to where a student lives, or their socio-economic status or the color of their skin. It is tied to those who see greatness in them and show them a mirror to see how great they are. This mirror is found in expectations, in coaching, in teaching, in learning, and in antiracist universally designed experiences. I expect greatness from each of you, first.

Each teacher and leader who is committed to the clarion call of educating our brilliant Black and Brown students has family and friends who think they are crazy for taking a chance to actually change the world. This is the start to a great catalogue of success stories. You know the names and faces of every driver you have empowered. My hope is this book will end where many of those great stories begin. This is the moment when you name each child, each circumstance, each story, statistic and stereotype and realize that their chance to drive and thrive starts with your decision to honor their greatness and teach them to drive by giving them an opportunity to truly learn how to learn.

10

Conclusions and Invitations

Consider this situation: Suppose you were on the side of the road with a flat tire. This is your first time encountering this situation, and you really don't know what to do. To make matters worse, you are on a country road, while there is just an hour or so of daylight remaining. Your children are in the car. You think to yourself, "I know that I should know how to change a tire, but I don't even know the first thing about the tools or where they are. I'm really stuck here."

You have a clear vision of where you want to go, but this circumstance is leaving you stranded, alone and responsible for others who are counting on you. Many passersby come and go. There is a steady stream of traffic. You reassure yourself that someone will help you eventually, right? There are passersby who stretch their necks to see what is happening. Some slow down just to assess the situation as they roll by. Others roll down their window to ask if you are okay, without even waiting for an answer. Still others pause just long enough to shout out the obvious, "It's just a flat tire! Change it and get out of the way!"

They are angry at the inconvenience your hardship is causing. One person actually gets out of the car and chastises you about the ridiculousness of not possessing the common sense to change a tire. Don't you drive every day? Whoever taught you to drive surely should have taught you how to take care of yourself on the road!" After administering the tongue lashing, that driver gets back in his car and leaves.

Another driver gets out and says, "Listen up. I'm going to teach you how to change a tire—all you do is this." He begins a masterful illustration of the wrenches and jacks and lug nuts that are second nature to him. With all eyes on him, he graciously announces, "Now you have everything you need to be successful in changing the tire." He takes off, having taught you a Tire Changing 101, which was perfectly accurate information, but you are still stuck on the side of the road, with the children and a flat tire. The sun is setting and there is very little time before you will be surrounded by complete darkness. You do have a few new vocabulary words, but you still have this dilemma.

Another car pulls up. "Hey are you, okay?"

You roll your eyes wondering if this is real help or not. "Just a flat tire," you say, almost robotically.

"Oh, no! There is never a good time for a flat tire. Are those your children? How old are they?"

"Yup they are mine. 10, 7, and 2."

"How long have you been out here, would they like a snack? My name is Dave. Nice to meet you." He pulls just in front of where your car is sitting and gets out. He stands just to the side of your car and asks, "Do you have roadside assistance? If not, I do, and I'll stay with you until we can get some help." You make small talk for about 20 minutes until assistance arrives.

You aren't sure at first whether he is trustworthy, but you realize you are desperate, and his help is a lot different from others you have encountered. When they get the car jacked up, he explains to you everything they are doing so that you have a better understanding. He asks if you would like to take a few pictures along the way, so that you will have them if you ever have to do this again. Now, the eloquent passersby lecture made at least a little more sense seeing things in action. The roadside assistant takes a moment to praise you. "Pulling over was the best way to handle this! Do you know how many people drive on a flat and damage the rim?"

You smile, glad that you didn't go too far. Dave had to ask the roadside assistant a few questions. "Heck, I learned a few new things today, too." He laughs. You know that he is asking questions for your benefit, but you appreciate his kindness in prompting your learning. Now you are sitting behind the wheel on three tires and a donut. You have enough to get you to your next destination, safely. You take a moment to reflect that just a few hours ago you were hopeless and helpless over just a spare tire; until the right person helped you make sense of the situation.

This situation is a parable of sorts. The driver—that is, the student—is struggling to find to get back on the road to their destination. The student doesn't just feel stranded. The student is stranded and desperate and isolated and alone. The student is surrounded by resources but does not know how to use them. The student has been criticized, labeled, left to their own devices, chastised, scolded, diminished, and made to disappear. This student has been identified as troubled, deficient, not up to par. The student does not have the skills to show what they know. The student agrees with all the notions that others propose. They never heard the word "DUMB," but the student has felt that way. So the student sits on the side of the educational road. And the student encounters you!

There is a difference when teachers honor their students by inviting them to show their brilliance. Yes, every child has an area of genius—a way in which they can shine. Utilizing UDL is literally pulling your car over to the side of the road where a child feels stuck and customizing your teaching to invite them in. The antiracist work is acknowledging the barriers that others don't speak of or address and annihilating them. This does not mean you will drive them to their destination, but rather that they will have all the tools they need to drive themselves. They may not have three children counting on them right now, but think of the opportunities you open up for them simply by empowering them with engagement, representation, action and expression that they can learn, they can grow, they can get to their destination.

When we allow the circumstances to be our catalyst students will dream with us for better. When we equip students with the tools to become experts at their own learning, then we silence the voices of criticism and negativity that may have become so loud that they are debilitating in a child's educational career. No matter where they are on the road, pulled over due to falling so far behind or feeling hopeless, trudging along with various misconceptions and failing grades, moving at a slow pace due to nonacademic barriers, or full speed ahead excelling despite all else—regardless of where they are on this road, educators can equip them with skills to accelerate, safely to destination graduation and beyond.

Indisposable Invitations to Learn

In this day of social media, the art of invitation has changed drastically. Wedding invitations and RSVPs have gone "digital." Social media invitation features allow you to invite massive amounts of people to one event. You lose that special feeling when you find out you are one of thousands who have been invited to an event. Looking at the list of invitees often makes me feel like my presence won't be noticed or missed. That invitation is then disposable. But, when an invitation is received that is customized, beautiful, and includes a personal note, I am more inclined to check my schedule and reciprocate the effort that has been communicated, so intentionally to me.

How do we craft learning experiences that communicate to every student we have thought carefully and intentionally about inviting them to learn with us? There are several things to consider when crafting a lesson with the UDL framework:

Who am I inviting to learn today?

Presenting options for how students consume content has to be strategic to be effective. Students have to have the space to reflect on the mode of content consumption by answering the questions, "How do you know that you are learning? How do you keep track of where you are and where you need to be? What do you do to make sure that you are putting feedback into use?" The most successful invitations to learning constantly embed the answer to the question "What's in it for me?" for both teacher and student. With the invitation, there is an accountability RSVP to ensure that learning is taking place.

Barbara McCombs (2010), a professor at the University of Denver, puts it this way: "When students understand their role as an agent (the one in charge) over their own feelings, thinking and learning behaviors, they are more likely to take responsibility for their learning. To be autonomous learners, however, students need to have some actual choice and control." Having choice helps students become responsible participants and co-creators in the educational process.

How can I communicate care in the lesson that I am teaching?

Think back to the parable for a moment. Remember the passerby who taught Tire Changing 101. He had all the facts, but he didn't really care to see that the learning was acquired or put into action. Did he care about you being stuck? Did he care about those who were depending on you being stuck? I'm not going to say he didn't care, but I will say that he did not communicate care with his words or actions. You can be intentional about communicating care while teaching. It is a part of a customized invitation of learning.

Vicki Zakrzewski (2012), director of education at the Greater Good Science Center at the University of California–Berkeley, reports on research showing that when teachers show students that they care, then students are academically more successful and also show greater "prosocial" and kind behavior. In the same blog post, she writes:

> A caring teacher can transform the school experience especially for students who face enormous difficulties, such as dropping out or dysfunctional home lives. One student who faced these kinds of hardships told a researcher that the greatest thing a teacher can do is to care and to understand. "Because if not," he said, "the kid will say, 'Oh, they're giving up on me, so I might as well give up on myself'."

Your care transforms the life of a student and every person they come in contact with.

What opportunities for input can I create to honor my students' voices individually and collectively?

Building learning communities where teachers and students learn together make such a difference. Students have preferences, they have areas of giftedness. Environments where learning is paramount means that questions are welcome, and that the teacher does not always have to have the answer. Students have the freedom and flexibility to speak and the skills and self regulation to listen to enhance the community's learning and not detract from it. As Marzano (2018) puts it: "Engaging student voice in classroom discussions deepens content knowledge and supports higher student achievement through constructing understanding and student engagement in learning."

How many means of representation can I bring to the lesson to give more learners access to the big ideas in this unit?

The CAST UDL Guidelines (2018) remind us that, "Learning is impossible if information is imperceptible to the learner, and difficult when information is presented in formats that require extraordinary effort or assistance. To reduce barriers to learning, it is important to ensure that key information is equally perceptible to all learners." Crafting an invitation that is universal enough to convey the same information but customized enough to feel personal is both art and science. To invite all students to the party of learning, think about how you display information and always offer an alternative to how it is displayed. If you have notes on the board, think about offering an audio version of the notes, or using graphical representations that will make the content stick. While you are teaching, build in support for varying learners—offer a glossary or a legend so that students can follow along or refer to it as needed. Formula sheets and symbols also provide support. Create "class hacks" as easy ways to remember the topics of the day.

What's in it for me?

Invite students to pack their learning and take it with them to other classes and bring back a report of how many connections to the content they could make in other classes in just one day. Helping students see the relationships and highlight the big ideas outside of your classroom will help them see that this invitation isn't just good for your class but opens up the walls of your classroom to the rest of the world. When we invite students utilizing multiple means of representation it honors their educational journey. When they see that the invitation is worthwhile, it will become mutually valued and treasured. Preparing for all students lets each one know that this learning experience is crafted for them personally, not just because their name appeared on your roster, but because you are passionate about their pursuit of excellence. Your teaching by invitation tells them:

1. I care enough to teach for you personally.

2. I care enough to learn from you with sincerity.

Reflection

- What role in the parable did you most identify with when you were a student?

- What role do you identify with as a teacher or leader? How about as a parent or as a child? What implications will this parable have on your teaching? Your learning? Your planning?

- How can you invite your students to learn? What are a few ways you want to try multiple means of representation?

Planning for variability is so critical in all learning environments because having a flexible learning environment allows all students to learn without having to shoehorn themselves into a one-size-fits-all system. We create a learning environment that is not only prepared for student differences but welcoming. Welcoming students of all variabilities takes on the task of creating an environment where student variability is not just tolerated, but rather celebrated. The building blocks of UDL lend themselves to high expectations and personalized pathways for all individual students, not for a mythical "average" student. Begin planning to invite their lights to shine in many different ways.

In her book *We Want to Do More Than Survive: Abolitionist Teaching and the Pursuit of Educational Freedom*, Bettina Love (2019) writes:

> Abolitionist teaching ensures that students feel safe in schools and that schools are not perpetrators of violence toward the very students they are supposed to protect. Abolitionist teaching is calling out your fellow teachers who degrade and diminish dark children and do not think dark children matter (pp. 11–12).

UDL captures the essence of safety for all students and antiracist teaching makes sure that the safety intended is protected for Black and Brown students. Implementing antiracist UDL practices will not be easy. But educational spaces will be better for our Black and Brown children who have been mishandled, misguided, and mistreated for as long as history has been recorded in America.

Our outcomes have begged us to make the changes to our justice systems, our community funding, and our educational practices. It is time to stand up for the brilliant Black and Brown students who are labeled, who slip through the cracks, who are dismissed and who are disappearing. Antiracist UDL practices are a commitment to stand with Black and Brown communities beyond lip service. It is a personal choice to stand for what is right.

My principal from elementary school, (who was my kindergarten teacher, and my mom's kindergarten teacher), had us memorize a pledge that we said every single day and it ends this way, "I promise to keep an open mind towards all people/To seek the goals of brotherhood/ To stand for what is right/ From now until judgment day. Right on." I made a promise and sealed it with a fist pump every single time I said the words, "Right on."

I made a promise to stand up for what is right. Before I even understood fully what was right, I was empowered with language that compelled me to take action.

Today, I think of those words often. These words are the soundtrack to ensuring a quality education for Black and Brown children. These words are the backdrop to decision making and professional development that dismantle racist systems one bite of the elephant at a time. As the words of my principal inspired me, it is my hope that my words will keep you up at night. That my words will draw you into this fight against injustice for Black and Brown students. I hope that you will find a community of antiracist UDL implementing warriors who use both their words and deed to prove to Black and Brown students that they matter. You cannot sit this one out. I need you. Every Black and Brown student needs you to fight!

Will you empower Black and Brown children to make their own decisions for their learning?

Will you give them a safe space for productive struggle, a place where they learn what to do when they make mistakes or fail or fall?

Will you give them support that does not cripple them, but rather strengthens them to reach higher and aim farther than society ever dared to imagine?

Will you release power and empower them to amplify their voices, their concerns, their choices and their destinations?

Will you believe in them enough to clear space from your agenda so they can make sense of barriers visible and invisible in the classroom, in the school systems, in their cities and in their world?

Will you let them drive, teaching them how to learn safely, how to protect their heart and minds and dreams?

Will you teach them when to slow up, how to pull over, how to use every resource they have, and how to know who is qualified to offer assistance?

Will you promise me you will not water down curriculum or sugarcoat world events?

Will you surround yourself with fighters who will check you and check on you?

Will you be aware of who you are and biases that get in the way of their learning?

Will you be aware of each learner and not paint them with one broad brush?

Will you get in their way if there is academic danger?

Will you get out of their way when they are ready to drive off into the sunset of success?

Will you teach them to drive their own learning and put them in the driver's seat?

Black and Brown children deserve an education that sets them up to hold the keys. Let them drive!

Controversy is born the moment dreamers begin taking actions to invite the marginalized ones into the secret society of success. It takes bravery to dream beyond the locked gates of educational access for all. It takes guts to create environments dedicated to academic success for Black and Brown children. It takes rebellion to protest the educational status quo by not just believing in an empowering educational journey for every Black and Brown learner but by living it, sharing it, cultivating it, and rebuking everyone who isn't striving for it. This group of rabble-rousing, barrier-eliminating, culture-busting wild men and women are the ones who will actualize the dream of access and success for all children.

And let's be clear, when we say "all" we need to be brave enough to identify the students who the system has not traditionally served. We know that our white, privileged students benefit most from the system as it was designed. It's more important than ever that we recognize that our systems are not socially just or equitable for our students with disabilities, our English language learners, our LGBTQ students, our students who experience trauma, students who are economically disadvantaged, and our Black and Brown students.

When all students are learning we will revitalize our cities, energize our economies, revolutionize our quality of life, invest in tomorrow, and enjoy a more beautiful today. Working to prepare the learning environment for every student to succeed is a simultaneous manifesto to ensure liberty, access, and excellence for all. To do this, we must not only implement the principles of Universal Design for Learning, but we must strive to create learning environments, systems and schools that are antiracist.

You have the tools.

You have the keys.

Drive.

Teach our Black and Brown babies to drive.

References

Aguilar, E. (2017). How to cultivate trust: Always remember 5 to 1. Blog post retrieved from http://brightmorningteam.com/2017/09/how-to-cultivate-trust-always-remember-5-to-1/

Ahram, R., Stembridge, A., Fergus, E., & Noguera, P. (2018). Framing urban school challenges: The problems to examine when implementing response to intervention. New York: RTI Action Network. Retrieved from www.rtinetwork.org/learn/diversity/urban-school-challenges

Barnard, B. (2017, January 28). Avoiding failure is bad for learning. *Concord Monitor*. Retrieved from https://www.concordmonitor.com/Avoiding-failure-7722659

Bindreiff, D. (2016). Mindsets impact perceptions of student behavior. Blog post retrieved from http://blog.mindsetworks.com/entry/behavior-is-learned

Bohrnstedt, G., Kitmitto, S., Ogut, B., Sherman, D., & Chan, D. (2015). NAEP Studies: School composition and the Black-white achievement gap. Washington, DC: National Center for Educational Statistics. Retrieved from https://nces.ed.gov/nationsreportcard/pubs/studies/2015018.aspx

Boschma, J. & Brownstein, R. (2016 , February). The concentration of poverty in American schools. *The Atlantic*. Retrieved from www.theatlantic.com/education/archive/2016/02/concentration-poverty-american-schools/471414/

Box of Crayons. (2015). Three habits to have your people with you, not against you. Blog post retrieved from https://boxofcrayons.com/2015/07/three-habits-to-have-your-people-with-you-not-against-you/

Budds, D. (2020, June 11). Harvard students are teaching Harvard how to be antiracist: And therein lies the problem. Online post retrieved from www.curbed.com/2020/6/11/21287866/harvard-gsd-students-antiracism

Camera, L. (2016, January 13). Achievement gap between white and black students still gaping. *US News & World Report.* Retrieved from www.usnews.com/news/blogs/data-mine/2016/01/13/achievement-gap-between-white-and-black-students-still-gaping

CAST. (2018a). UDL and asssessment. Online post retrieved from http://udloncampus.cast.org/page/assessment_udl#.W1UiG9VKipo

CAST (2018b). *Universal Design for Learning Guidelines version 2.0.* Wakefield, MA: Author.

Centers for Disease Control. (2020). Hospitalization rates and characteristics of patients hospitalized with laboratory-confirmed coronavirus disease 2019. Atlanta, GA: Author.

Coleman, J. S., United States., & National Center for Education Statistics. (1966). Equality of educational opportunity [summary report]. Washington: National Center for Educational Statistics.

Cook, L. (2015, January 28). U.S. education: Still separate and unequal. *US News & World Report.* Retrieved from www.usnews.com/news/blogs/data-mine/2015/01/28/us-education-still-separate-and-unequal

Delpit, L. (1988). The silenced dialogue: Power and pedagogy in educating other people's children. *Harvard Educational Review, 58*(3), 280–299. DOI:10.17763/haer.58.3.c43481778r528qw4

Ertmer, P. & Newby T. (1996). The expert learner: Strategic, self-regulated and reflective. *Instructional Science, 24*, 1–24.

Eshet-Alkali, Y., & Amichai-Hamburger, Y. (2004). Experiments in digital literacy. *CyberPsychology & Behavior 7*(4), 421–429. DOI: 10.1089/cpb.2004.7.421

Fantz, A. (2015, April 15). Prison time for some Atlanta school educators in cheating scandal. *CNN.* Retrieved from www.cnn.com/2015/04/14/us/georgia-atlanta-public -schools-cheating-scandal-verdicts/index.html

Fiock, H. & Garcia, H. (2019, November 8). How to give your students better feedback with technology. *Chronicle of Higher Education.* Retrieved from www.chronicle.com/interactives /20191108-Advice-Feedback

Goddard, R., Hoy, W., & Hoy, A. (2004). Collective efficacy beliefs: Theoretical developments, empirical evidence, and future direction. *Educational Researcher 33*(3), 3–13. DOI: 10.3102/0013189X033003003.

Gratz, D. B. (2009). The problem with performance pay. *Educational Leadership 63*(3), 76–79.

Hammond, Z. (2014). *Culturally responsive teaching and the brain: Promoting authentic engagement and rigor among culturally and linguistically diverse students.* Thousand Oaks, CA: Corwin.

Hays, B. (2015, April 17). MIT study links family income, test scores, brain anatomy. *United Press International.* Retrieved from www.upi.com/Science_News/2015/04/17/MIT-study -links-family-income-test-scores-brain-anatomy /4491429283732/

Hopkins, G. (2015). How can teachers develop students' motivation—and success? *Education World.* Retrieved from www.educationworld.com/a_issues/chat/chat010.shtml

Jensen, E. (2009). *Teaching with poverty in mind: What being poor does to kids' brains and what schools can do about it.* Alexandria, VA: ASCD. Retrieved from www.ascd.org/publications /books/109074/chapters/Understanding-the-Nature -of-Poverty.aspx

Joining Forces for Children (2020). 10 ACEs, as identified by the CDC-Kaiser study. Blog post retrieved from www. joiningforcesforchildren.org/what-are-aces/

Keels, M. (2018, March 23). Supporting students with chronic trauma. *Edutopia.* Retrieved from www.edutopia.org/article /supporting-students-chronic-trauma

Killian, S. (2017). Hattie effect size 2016 update. Blog post retrieved from www.evidencebasedteaching.org.au/hattie -effect-size-2016-update/

Kozol, J. (1991). *Savage inequalities: Children in America's schools.* New York: Crown.

Lippman. L., Burns, S. & McArthur, E. (1996). *Urban schools: The challenge of location and poverty.* Washington, DC: National Center for Education Statistics.

Littlepythagoras. (2012). Audri's Rube Goldberg monster trap. YouTube video retrieved from www.youtube.com/watch? v=0uDDEEHDf1Y

Love, B. (2019). *We want to do more than survive: Abolitionist teaching and the pursuit of educational freedom.* Boston: Beacon Press.

Marzano, R. J., (2018). Tips from Dr. Marzano: Delivering on the promise. Blog post retrieved from www.marzanoresearch .com/resources/tips/dotp_tips_archive#tip2

McCombs, B., (2010). Developing responsible and autonomous learners: A key to motivating students. Washington, DC: American Psychological Association. Retrieved from www .apa.org/education/k12/learners.aspx

Meyer, A., Rose, D. H., & Gordon, D. (2014). *Universal design for learning: Theory and practice.* Wakefield, MA: CAST Professional Publishing.

National Assessment of Educational Progress. (2015). NAEP studies: School composition and the Black-white achievement gap. Retrieved from https://nces.ed.gov /nationsreportcard/pubs/studies/2015018.aspx

Najavits, L. (2019). *Finding your best self: Recovery from trauma, addiction, or both.* New York: Guilford Press.

National Center on Cultural and Linguistic Responsiveness. (2019). Exploring cultural concepts: Funds of knowledge handout. Retrieved from https://eclkc.ohs.acf.hhs.gov/sites /default/files/pdf/spring2spring-funds-of-knowledge-eng .pdf

National Center for Injury Prevention and Control: Division of Violence Prevention. (2019). Preventing adverse childhood experiences (ACEs): Leveraging the best available evidence. Retrieved from www.cdc.gov/violenceprevention/pdf /preventingACES.pdf

Nelson, J. (2006). *Positive discipline: The classic guide to helping children develop self-discipline, responsibility, cooperation, and problem-solving skills.* New York: Ballantine.

Nieto, S. (2004). *Affirming diversity: The sociopolitical context of multicultural education.* New York: Pearson.

Novak, K. (2014). Scaffold listening and speaking the UDL way. Blog post retrieved from www.novakeducation.com /scaffold-speaking-listening-udl-way/

Novak, K. (2016). *UDL Now!: A teacher's guide to applying Universal Design for Learning in today's classrooms.* Wakefield, MA: CAST Professional Publishing.

Pitney, N. (2015, October 21). How to give your child the gift of failure. *Huffington Post.* Blog post retrieved from

www.huffpost.com/entry/give-the-gift-of-failure_n
_5627c092e4b08589ef4a20cb

Reardon, S. F., Robinson-Cimpian, J. P., & Weathers, E. S. (2015). Patterns and trends in racial/ethnic and socioeconomic academic achievement gaps. In H. Ladd & M. Goertz (Eds). *Handbook of research in education finance and policy* (2nd Ed., pp. 491–509). Mahwah, NJ: Lawrence Erlbaum.

Rose, D. H., & Gravel, J. W. (2009). Getting from here to there: UDL, global positioning systems, and lessons for improving education. In D. T. Gordon, J. W. Gravel, & L. A. Schifter (Eds.), *A policy reader in Universal Design for Learning* (pp. 5–18). Cambridge, MA: Harvard Education Press.

Saw, G., Schneider, B., Frank, K., Chen, I., Keesler, V., & Martineau, J. (2017). The impact of being labeled as a persistently lowest achieving school: Regression discontinuity evidence on consequential school labeling. *American Journal of Education,123*(4), 585–613. doi:10.1086/692665

Schulten, K. (2017, December 7). Making It relevant: Helping students connect their studies to the world today. *New York Times.* Retrieved from www.nytimes.com/2017/12/07 /learning/lesson-plans/making-it-relevant-helping -students-connect-their-studies-to-the-world-today.html

Stanier, M.B. (2016). *The coaching habit: Say less, ask more and change the way you lead forever.* Vancouver: Page Two Books.

Sturgis, C. (2017). Laying the foundation for competency education with culture and climate. Blog post retrieved from www.gettingsmart.com/2017/03/laying-the-foundation -for-competency-education-with-culture-and-climate/

Tatum, B. D. (2003). *"Why are all the Black kids sitting together in the cafeteria?" and other conversations about race.* New York: Basic Books.

Urban Education Institute. (2017). Practicing trauma-responsive teaching. Brief retrieved from https://uei.uchicago.edu/news/article/practicing-trauma-responsive-teaching

U.S. Department of Education (2019). *Chronic absenteeism in the nation's schools: A hidden crisis.* Washington, DC: Author. Retrieved from www2.ed.gov/datastory/chronic absenteeism.html

Vygotsky, L. S. (1978). *Mind in society: The development of higher psychological processes.* Cambridge, MA: Harvard University Press.

Wade, R., Shea, J. A., Rubin, D., & Wood, J. (2014). Adverse childhood experiences of low-income urban youth. *Pediatrics, 134*(1), e13–e20; DOI: https://doi.org/10.1542/peds.2013-2475

Zakrewski, V. (2012). Four ways teachers can show they care. Blog post retrieved from https://greatergood.berkeley.edu/article/item/caring_teacher_student_relationship

Zemelman, S., Daniels, H., & Hyde, A. A. (2012). *Best practice: Bringing standards to life in America's classrooms.* Portsmouth, NH: Heinemann.

Index

Acknowledgements

God whispered a dream to my heart in second grade to become a writer. I thank God for the dream come true that this project is. I dedicate this book to Tamir Rice for his brilliance that came through in his expression of arts and athletics. You will never be forgotten. We will fight for your light to shine, always. Special thanks to Samaria Rice for teaching us how to stand for what is right. Thank you for lending your voice to the struggle and to this book. I appreciate you.

This book is for educators of Black and Brown students, especially those of you who have committed your lives to serving in urban schools. You are battle tested, combat ready, and always poised to fight. You are the soldiers who take the learning lamp of education into the places that are forgotten, silenced and marginalized. You matter! I know that you are weary, sometimes angry and on the edge of losing it, but this book is for you. You are effective, encouraging, persistent, resistant, and resilient.

This book is also for our Black and Brown students, especially my EC babies. My dream for you is that classrooms will be engaging, pushing you toward excellence in every way possible. I want to see you shine, read your writing, hear your songs, see your heart in your work. You deserve excellence, and this is my way of keeping the promise I made to you in 2001 when I started this work. I will fight for your honor because I know that your honor is worth fighting for.

To my mentor and my friend, Katie Novak, EdD, words cannot express the gratitude I have for you. Thank you for locking arms with me and dreaming and working for equity and excellence everywhere. You are a rare gem and your brilliance lights up the world!

Thank you to David Gordon of CAST Professional Publishing. I can't put into adequate words how much of a catalyst your encouragement and wisdom has been, but I can tell you how grateful for you I am. Thank you Sue Miller Wiltz for adding your joy and expertise to this project. Much gratitude goes to the entire staff of CAST Professional Publishing. You have been a joy to work with and grow with as we fight inequity together!

To Lindie Johnson for your beautiful art that graces the cover of this book. Thank you for turning an idea into a reality.

To my Tony, Lani, and Tony Jr.—you are gifts that teach me so much love, light, and growth. I hope you hear your influence in these pages. Thank you for listening to my talks, reading my chapters, engaging in my rants, refining my intense love for analogies and sharing this journey with me. The world is enriched because you are here. I love you all!

To Mommy Antoinette, Daddy William, Grandma Marsh, Grandma Rogers, Mama Steph, Dad Tony, and Mama Sandra.

To Bianca, Nikky, Kandi, Stephen, and Christina.

For Auntie Verlana, Auntie Shaundallah, Uncle Hassan, Uncle Raheem, and Uncle Doni.

For Amanda, Mildred, Ceola, Eaton, and Hattie—your legacy has led me.

For Gwendolyn and Langston—We Real Cool and I, Too Sing!

To Lydia Harris, Stephanie Tome, Madeline Harland, Beatriz Cunningham, Linda Kuhn, Chris Mominey, Marty Poluse, Bertha Ealy, Charlene Dayton, Bill Raddell, Leola "Grandma" Wilson.

To my family, friends, and supporters

To my sister circle and my sorors.

To my Bestest Cheryll and Bestie Joanna.

To Dr. Peterman, Dr. Zenkov, and Dr. Corley.
To Byron, Henry, Paula, Courtney, Tom, Kevin, and Dennis.
To every single "Munn"ster EVER—this is your story.
To my EC family.
To the 216!
To my UDL peeps.
We dream together! We achieve together! We fight together!

About the Author

Andratesha Fritzgerald, EdS, serves as Director of Teaching, Learning and Innovation for the East Cleveland (OH) City School Districts and has been a teacher and leader in urban schools for nearly 20 years. Her life's work is to awaken, celebrate and activate the brilliance of teachers, leaders, and students to actualize achievement wherever it seems impossible.

Anita Louise Photography

She has been a speaker at CAST's annual UDL Symposium and state conferences for teachers, and is a keynote speaker and professional development provider with Novak Educational Consulting. A self-proclaimed *Jeopardy* enthusiast and imagination expert, she loves writing and dreaming out loud with her husband, two children, and committed educators who believe in academic success for all.

About Samaria Rice

As a mother of social justice, activist, and the founder and CEO of the Tamir Rice, Ms. Samaria Rice proudly serves as an advocate for juvenile rights in Cleveland, Ohio. Since the murder of her 12-year-old son Tamir by Cleveland Police  in 2014, Ms. Rice has committed her life to justice and standing on the frontlines for children.

Samaria's passion for civil rights reaches across lines of difference, uniting us all to work towards change. Following Tamir's death, Samaria has continued to use her voice in the service of her son's legacy. Samaria encourages us to take back our communities by standing up for justice. She has become a motivating force for families and communities across the nation.

Ms. Rice founded the Tamir Rice Foundation in 2016. The mission of the Foundation is to invest in the growth and enrichment of children through the arts and to create a world in which all children feel safe, nurtured, and valued—especially in their darkest times. Ms. Rice is active in the arts nationally and globally. She frequently collaborates with artists and arts organizations on projects in response to the shooting of Tamir, state-sanctioned violence, and juvenile rights.

Her biggest undertaking yet is the Tamir Rice Afrocentric Cultural Center, which will provide artistic, educational, and civic programs for youth while celebrating the history and culture of people of African descent. he was recently featured on *Essence's* 2019 Woke 100 list alongside changemakers such as Michelle Obama, Ava Duvernay, and Gayle King.

Please visit https://www.tamirricefoundation.org